THE BEST JOKE BOOK IN THE WORLD EVER!

IMAGINE THAT

Licensed exclusively to Imagine That Publishing Ltd
Tide Mill Way, Woodbridge, Suffolk, IP12 1AP, UK
www.imaginethat.com
Copyright © 2018 Imagine That Group Ltd
All rights reserved
0 2 4 6 8 9 7 5 3 1
Manufactured in China

Knock Knock!
Who's there?
Dr.
Dr. Who?
You just said it!

Knock Knock!
Who's there?
Luke.
Luke who?
Luke through the keyhole and find out!

Knock Knock!
Who's there?
Ammonia.
Ammonia who?
Ammonia little girl and I can't reach the doorbell!

Knock Knock!
Who's there?
Ice cream.
Ice cream who?
Ice cream loudly!

Knock Knock!
Who's there?
Heywood.
Heywood who?
Heywood you open the door!

Knock Knock!
Who's there?
Yah.
Yah who?
Are you a cowboy or something?

Knock Knock!
Who's there?
Lettuce.
Lettuce who?
Lettuce in!

Knock Knock!
Who's there?
Onya.
Onya who?
Onya marks, get set, go!

Doctor, doctor, I keep thinking I'm a dog.

How long have you felt this way?

Ever since I was a puppy.

Doctor, doctor, you have to help me out.

Certainly, which way did you come in?

Doctor, doctor, everyone ignores me.

Next!

4

Doctor, doctor, the Invisible Man is in reception.

Tell him I can't see him right now.

Doctor, doctor, I keep thinking I'm a pair of curtains.

Pull yourself together, man.

Doctor, doctor, I feel like a doorbell.

Take two pills and give me a ring.

What do you call a
guard with 100 legs?

A sentrypede!

What do cows like to
dance to?

Any kind of moosic.

What books do
chickens read?

Yolk books.

What's the best
way to stop milk
from going off?

Leaving it inside
the cow.

Why was the centipede late?

Because he was playing 'This Little Piggy' with his baby brother!

What do you get if you cross a centipede and a chicken?

Enough drumsticks to feed an army!

What did one centipede say to the other centipede?

'You've got a lovely pair of legs, You've got a lovely pair of legs ...!'

What did the earwig say as it fell down the stairs?

'Ear we go!'

Knock Knock!
Who's there?
Perry.
Perry who?
Perry well, thank you!

Knock Knock!
Who's there?
Summer.
Summer who?
**Summer good,
summer bad!**

Knock Knock!
Who's there?
Ivana.
Ivana who?
Ivana be alone!

Knock Knock!
Who's there?
Carmen.
Carmen who?
Carmen get it!

Knock Knock!
Who's there?
Thumping.
Thumping who?
Thumping green and slimy just crawled up your leg!

Knock Knock!
Who's there?
Ooze.
Ooze who?
Ooze that knocking on my door?

Knock Knock!
Who's there?
Scott.
Scott who?
Scott nothing to do with you!

Knock Knock!
Who's there?
Boo.
Boo who?
Don't cry!

9

Doctor, doctor, I keep thinking that I'm shrinking.

Now, settle down. You'll just have to be a little patient.

Doctor, doctor, I have a rash that looks like a bowl of strawberries.

I'm sure I have some cream for that.

Doctor, doctor, I broke my leg in two places.

Stay out of those places.

Doctor, doctor, sometimes I think I'm a wigwam and sometimes I think I'm a teepee.

I know your problem — you're two tents.

Why did Dr Cyclops give up teaching?

Because he only had one pupil.

Doctor, doctor, I feel like a sheep.

Oh dear, that's baaaaaaaaaad!

Knock Knock!
Who's there?
Doris.
Doris who?
Doris locked, that's why I had to knock!

Knock Knock!
Who's there?
Toby.
Toby who?
Toby or not to be, that is the question!

Knock Knock!
Who's there?
Snow.
Snow who?
Snow good asking me!

Knock Knock!
Who's there?
Tank.
Tank who?
You're welcome!

12

Knock Knock!
Who's there?
Caesar.
Caesar who?
Caesar jolly good fellow!

Knock Knock!
Who's there?
Keith.
Keith who?
Keith me and find out!

Knock Knock!
Who's there?
Arthur.
Arthur who?
Arthur moment and I'll go round the back!

Knock Knock!
Who's there?
Olive.
Olive who?
Olive you!

Knock Knock!
Who's there?
Harry.
Harry who?
Harry up and open the door!

Knock Knock!
Who's there?
Anita.
Anita who?
Anita hug!

Knock Knock!
Who's there?
Oliver.
Oliver who?
Oliver across the road from you!

Knock Knock!
Who's there?
Hawaii.
Hawaii who?
I'm fine! Hawaii you?

Knock Knock!
Who's there?
Grandma. Knock knock!
Who's there?
Grandma. Knock Knock!
Who's there?
Grandma. Knock Knock!
Who's there?
Aunt.
Aunt who?
**Aunt you glad
Grandma's gone?**

Knock Knock!
Who's there?
Ben.
Ben who?
**Ben wondering
what you're up to!**

Knock Knock!
Who's there?
**Control freak.
Now you say,
'control freak who?'**

Doctor, doctor,
I keep thinking I'm a cowboy.
How long have you felt like that?
About a yeeeehaaah!

Doctor, doctor, I tend to
flush a lot.

Don't worry, it's just a
chain reaction.

Doctor, doctor, I keep
thinking I'm a bee.

Buzz off!

Doctor, doctor, the pills you gave me for my smelly armpits don't work.

What's wrong with them?

They keep slipping out from under my arms.

Doctor, doctor, I've got bad teeth, foul breath and smelly feet.

Sounds like you've got foot and mouth disease.

Doctor, doctor, my husband smells like fish.

Poor sole.

Knock Knock!
Who's there?
Shelby.
Shelby who?
Shelby coming round the mountain when she comes!

Knock Knock!
Who's there?
Island.
Island who?
Island on Earth three days ago!

Knock Knock!
Who's there?
Woo.
Woo hoo?
Don't get so excited, it's just a joke!

Knock Knock!
Who's there?
Pecan.
Pecan who?
Pecan on someone your own size!

Knock Knock!
Who's there?
Gorilla.
Gorilla who?
Gorilla some cheese on toast please!

Knock Knock!
Who's there?
Aardvark.
Aardvark who?
Aardvark a million miles for one of your smiles!

Knock Knock!
Who's there?
Cows go.
Cows go who?
No! Cows go moo!

Knock Knock!
Who's there?
Annie.
Annie who?
Annie thing you can do I can do better!

Knock Knock!
Who's there?
Phyllis.
Phyllis who?
Phyllis up a glass of water!

Knock Knock!
Who's there?
Thistle.
Thistle who?
Thistle have to do until dinner's ready!

Knock Knock!
Who's there?
Police.
Police who?
Police stop telling these awful jokes!

Knock Knock!
Who's there?
Mary lee.
Mary lee who?
Mary lee we roll along!

Knock Knock!
Who's there?
Ray.
Ray who?
Ray-member me?

Knock Knock!
Who's there?
Plug.
Plug who?
Help, I'm going down the plug hole!

Knock Knock!
Who's there?
Hippo.
Hippo who?
Hippo birthday to you.
Hippo birthday to you!

Knock Knock!
Who's there?
Budgie.
Budgie who?
Budgie up, I want to squeeze in!

Doctor, doctor, I keep thinking I'm a caterpillar.

Don't worry, you'll soon change!

Doctor, doctor, I'm a burglar.

Have you taken anything for it?

Doctor, doctor, I keep thinking I'm a spider.

What a web of lies.

Doctor, doctor, you've taken out my tonsils, my adenoids, my gall bladder, and my appendix, but I still don't feel well.

That's quite enough out of you.

Doctor, doctor, I feel like a dog.

Sit!

Doctor, doctor, my baby is the image of his father.

Never mind — just so long as he's healthy.

Knock Knock!
Who's there?
Ali.
Ali who?
Ali cat!

Knock Knock!
Who's there?
Andrew.
Andrew who?
Andrew all over the wall!

Knock Knock!
Who's there?
Repeat.
Repeat who?
Who who who!

Knock Knock!
Who's there?
Amos.
Amos who?
Amosquito bit me!

24

Knock Knock!
Who's there?
Janet.
Janet who?
Janet a big fish?

Knock Knock!
Who's there?
Nobel.
Nobel who?
**Nobel, that's
why I knocked!**

Knock Knock!
Who's there?
Sarah.
Sarah who?
**Sarah a doctor
in the house?**

Knock Knock!
Who's there?
Dot.
Dot who?
**Dot's for me to know
and you to find out!**

Knock Knock!
Who's there?
Turkey.
Turkey who?
Turkey to the right, then it'll open!

Knock Knock!
Who's there?
Moo.
Moo who?
Make up your mind, are you a cow or an owl?

Knock Knock!
Who's there?
Giraffe.
Giraffe who?
Giraffe anything to eat, I'm starving!

Knock Knock!
Who's there?
Bison.
Bison who?
Bison new handles, these don't work!

26

Knock Knock!
Who's there?
Theodore.
Theodore who?
**Theodore is stuck
and it won't open!**

Knock Knock!
Who's there?
Wilma.
Wilma who?
**Wilma suppor
be ready soon?**

Knock Knock!
Who's there?
Cargo.
Cargo who?
Cargo beep beep!

Knock Knock!
Who's there?
Kanga.
Kanga who?
No, Kangeroo!

Doctor, doctor, I've lost my memory.

When did this happen?

When did what happen?

Doctor, doctor, I think I'm a rubber band.

Why don't you stretch yourself out on the couch and tell me all about it?

Doctor, doctor, everyone thinks I'm a liar.

I don't believe you.

Doctor, doctor, I think I'm an electric eel.

That's shocking.

Doctor, doctor, I need something to keep my falling hair in.

What about a bag?

Doctor, doctor, I keep seeing double.

Please sit on the couch.

Which one?

Doctor, doctor, I keep seeing an insect everywhere.

Don't worry — it's just a bug that's going around.

Knock Knock!
Who's there?
Icon.
Icon who?
Icon tell you another knock knock joke. Do you want me to?

Knock Knock!
Who's there?
Despair.
Despair who?
Despair tyre is flat!

Knock Knock!
Who's there?
Vitamin.
Vitamin who?
Vitamin for a party!

Knock Knock!
Who's there?
I used.
I used who?
I used to be able to reach the doorbell!

Knock Knock!
Who's there?
Hans!
Hans who?
Hans off my dog!

Knock Knock!
Who's there?
Claws!
Claws who?
Claws the door behind you!

Knock Knock!
Who's there?
Noise.
Noise who?
Noise to see you!

Knock Knock!
Who's there?
Neil.
Neil who?
Neil down and pet this cat!

What do you call a grasshopper with no legs?

A grasshover!

Why is it better to be a grasshopper than a cricket?

Because grasshoppers can play cricket, but crickets can't play grasshopper!

What's a teddy bear's favourite pasta?

Tagliateddy!

What is green and brown, has four legs and can kill you if it falls out of a tree and lands on you?

A bear on a branch.

32

What happened to the man who turned into an insect?

He just beetled off!

What is the insect's favourite game?

Cricket!

What's an insect's best chat-up line?

'Pardon me, but is this stool taken?'

What has four wheels and flies?

A rubbish bin!

Doctor, doctor, I think I'm a moth.

Get out of the way, you're in my light.

Doctor, doctor, I keep thinking I'm a needle.

I'm sorry, I don't see your point.

Doctor, doctor, I have amnesia.

Well, take these pills — you'll soon forget about it.

Doctor, doctor, I'm
having trouble with my
breathing.

I'll give you something
that will soon put
a stop to that.

Doctor, doctor, what
did the X-ray of my
head show?

Absolutely nothing.

Doctor, doctor, I'm
really ugly! What can I
do about it?

Hire yourself out for
Halloween parties.

Knock Knock!
Who's there?
Radio.
Radio who?
Radio not, here I come!

Knock Knock!
Who's there?
Omelette.
Omelette who?
Omelette smarter than you!

Knock Knock!
Who's there?
Justin.
Justin who?
Justin time for tea!

Knock Knock!
Who's there?
Maida.
Maida who?
Maida force be with you!

Knock Knock!
Who's there?
Egbert.
Egbert who?
Egbert no bacon, please!

Knock Knock!
Who's there?
Turnip.
Turnip who?
Turnip to school tomorrow or you'll be expelled!

Knock Knock!
Who's there?
Jess.
Jess who?
Jess me!

Knock Knock!
Who's there?
Ach.
Ach who?
Bless you!

Knock Knock!
Who's there?
Accordion.
Accordion who?
Accordion to the TV, it's going to rain tomorrow!

Knock Knock!
Who's there?
Ivor.
Ivor who?
Ivor message for you!

Knock Knock!
Who's there?
Wendy.
Wendy who?
Wendy wind blows the cradle will rock!

Knock Knock!
Who's there?
Soup.
Soup who?
Souperman!

Knock Knock!
Who's there?
Value.
Value who?
Value be my Valentine?

Knock Knock!
Who's there?
Abbey.
Abbey who?
Abbey stung me on the nose!

Knock Knock!
Who's there?
Shirley.
Shirley who?
Shirley you know my name by now!

Knock Knock!
Who's there?
Wales.
Wales who?
Wales as long as I'm here, let's go out!

Doctor, doctor,
I keep painting myself gold.

Don't worry — it's just a gilt
complex.

Doctor, doctor, I can't get
to sleep.

Sit on the edge of the bed
and you'll soon drop off.

Doctor, doctor,
I think I'm a
python.

You can't get
round me like
that, you know.

Doctor: I think you should
give up singing.

Patient: Why? Is it bad for
my health?

Doctor: No – you just sound awful.

Doctor, doctor, I think I'm
a bridge.

What's come over you?

Two cars, a large truck
and a coach.

Knock Knock!
Who's there?
Butter.
Butter who?
I butter not tell you!

Knock Knock!
Who's there?
Rotten egg.
Rotten egg who?
Splat! The yolks on you!

Knock Knock!
Who's there?
Red Denny.
Red Denny who?
Red Denny good books lately?

Knock Knock!
Who's there?
Wanda.
Wanda who?
Wanda know, then open the door!

Knock Knock!
Who's there?
Sacha.
Sacha who?
Sacha fuss because I knocked on your door!

Knock Knock!
Who's there?
Isabelle.
Isabelle who?
Isabelle necessary on your door?

Knock Knock!
Who's there?
Wayne.
Wayne who?
Wayne, wayne go away, come again another day!

Knock Knock!
Who's there?
Safari.
Safari who?
Safari so good!

Knock Knock!
Who's there?
P.
P who?
Well, thanks for telling me I smell!

Knock Knock!
Who's there?
Bow.
Bow who?
Not bow who, bow wow!

Knock Knock!
Who's there?
Orange.
Orange who?
Orange you going to open the door?

Knock Knock!
Who's there?
Flea.
Flea who?
Flea from that dog before he bites you!

44

Knock Knock!
Who's there?
Igloo.
Igloo who?
Igloo knew Steven
like I knew Steven!

Knock Knock!
Who's there?
Mister.
Mister who?
Mister last train!

Knock Knock!
Who's there?
Water.
Water who?
Water you doing
in my house!

Knock Knock!
Who's there?
Pooch.
Pooch who?
Pooch your arms
around me!

Doctor, doctor,
I think I'm a moth.

So why did you come here then?

Well, I saw this light at the window ...

Doctor, doctor, I got
pains in one eye when I
drink coffee.

Have you tried taking
the spoon out?

Doctor, doctor, I feel like
a spoon.

Well sit still and don't stir!

Doctor, doctor, have you got something for a bad headache?

Of course, take this hammer and hit yourself on the head.
Then you'll have a bad headache.

Doctor, doctor, I feel like a pack of cards.

I'll deal with you later.

Doctor, doctor, I keep thinking there are two of me.

One at a time please!

Knock Knock!
Who's there?
Nanna.
Nanna who?
Nanna your business!

Knock Knock!
Who's there?
Witches.
Witches who?
Witches the way home?

Knock Knock!
Who's there?
Ralph.
Ralph who?
Ralph! Ralph! Ralph! I'm a dog!

Knock Knock!
Who's there?
Pig.
Pig who?
Pig up your feet or you'll trip up!

Knock Knock!
Who's there?
Celia.
Celia who?
Celia later alligator, don't forget your toilet paper!

Knock Knock!
Who's there?
Saffron.
Saffron who?
Saffron a chair and it collapsed!

Knock Knock!
Who's there?
Larva.
Larva who?
Larva cup of tea!

Knock Knock!
Who's there?
Wooden shoe.
Wooden shoe who?
Wooden shoe like to know!

Knock Knock!
Who's there?
Harley.
Harley who?
Harley see you anymore!

Knock Knock!
Who's there?
Ray.
Ray who?
Ray-ning cats and dogs!

Knock Knock!
Who's there?
Ida.
Ida who?
Ida know, sorry!

Knock Knock!
Who's there?
Wade.
Wade who?
Wade till next time!

Knock Knock!
Who's there?
Alvin.
Alvin who?
**Alvin a great time,
how about you?**

Knock Knock!
Who's there?
Haden.
Haden who?
Haden seek!

Knock Knock!
Who's there?
Galway.
Galway who?
**Galway, you
bother me!**

Knock Knock!
Who's there?
Waiter.
Waiter who?
**Waiter minute while
I tie my shoe!**

Doctor, doctor, will this ointment clear up my spots?

I never make rash promises.

Doctor, doctor, I feel like a racehorse.

Take one of these every four laps.

Doctor, doctor, my sister here thinks she's invisible.

What sister?

Doctor, doctor, I'm on a diet and it's making me angry. Yesterday I bit someone's ear off.

Oh dear, that's a lot of calories.

Doctor, doctor, I'm boiling up.

Just simmer down.

Doctor, doctor, can I have a second opinion?

Of course, come back tomorrow!

Knock Knock!
Who's there?
Figs.
Figs who?
Figs the doorbell because it's broken!

Knock Knock!
Who's there?
Handsome.
Handsome who?
Handsome of that pizza to me!

Knock Knock!
Who's there?
Isadore.
Isadore who?
Isadore always that hard to knock on?

Knock Knock!
Who's there?
Wine.
Wine who?
Wine don't you like these jokes?

54

Knock Knock!
Who's there?
Avocado.
Avocado who?
Avocado cold!

Knock Knock!
Who's there?
Eyesore!
Eyesore who?
Eyesore do like you!

Knock Knock!
Who's there?
Candace.
Candace who?
Candace be the last knock knock joke?

Knock Knock!
Who's there?
Sam.
Sam who?
Sam person who knocked on the door last time!

Knock Knock!
Who's there?
Venice.
Venice who?
Venice your mother coming home?

Knock Knock!
Who's there?
Al.
Al who?
Al give you a kiss if you open the door!

Knock Knock!
Who's there?
Alfie.
Alfie who?
Alfie terrible if you leave!

Knock Knock!
Who's there?
Canoe.
Canoe who?
Canoe lend me some money?

Knock Knock!
Who's there?
Waddle.
Waddle who?
Waddle you give me if I go away?

Knock Knock!
Who's there?
Lass.
Lass who?
That's what cowboys do, isn't it?

Knock Knock!
Who's there?
Ike.
Ike who?
Ike can't stop laughing!

Knock Knock!
Who's there?
Thermos.
Thermos who?
Thermos be a better joke than this!

Doctor, doctor,
I keep thinking I'm God.

When did this start?

Well first I created the Sun,
then the Earth ...

Doctor, doctor,
I keep thinking I'm
invisible.

Who said that?

Doctor, doctor,
I keep thinking I'm
a vampire.

Necks please.

58

Doctor, doctor,
I keep thinking I'm a snake
about to shed its skin.

Go behind the screen and
slip into something more
comfortable.

Doctor, doctor, I feel
like an apple.

We must get to the
core of this.

Doctor, doctor, I
think I'm a yo-yo.

Are you stringing
me along?

What dog wears contact lenses?

A cock-eyed spaniel!

What is a dog's favourite flower?

Anything in your garden!

What's a dog's favourite hobby?

Collecting fleas!

How many seasons are there in a dog's life?

Just one, the moulting season!

Why is it called a 'litter' of puppies?

Because they mess up the whole house!

How do you stop a dog smelling?

Put a peg on its nose!

What is the best time to take a rottweiler for a walk?

Any time he wants to!

When does a dog go 'moo'?

When it is learning a new language!

Knock Knock!
Who's there?
Alfred.
Alfred who?
**Alfred the needle
if you sew!**

Knock Knock!
Who's there?
Aesop.
Aesop who?
**Aesop I saw a
puddy cat!**

Knock Knock!
Who's there?
Alec.
Alec who?
Alec my lolly!

Knock Knock!
Who's there?
Veal chop.
Veal chop who?
**Veal chop around and
see what bargains
we can find!**

Knock Knock!
Who's there?
Foster.
Foster who?
Foster than a speeding bullet!

Knock Knock!
Who's there?
Haden!
Haden who?
Haden in the bushes!

Knock Knock!
Who's there?
Sabina!
Sabina who?
Sabina long time since I saw you!

Knock Knock!
Who's there?
Sara.
Sara who?
Sara no other way into this building?

Doctor: You need new glasses.

Patient: How do you know? I haven't told you what's wrong with me yet.

I could tell as soon as you walked in through the window.

Doctor, doctor, I think I'm a snail.

Don't worry — we'll soon have you out of your shell.

Doctor, doctor, I keep thinking I'm a nit.

Will you get out of my hair?

Doctor, doctor, I think
I'm a butterfly.

Will you say what
you mean and stop
flying about?

Doctor, doctor,
I think I'm an adder.

Great. Can you help me with
my accounts then please?

Doctor, doctor, I
think I'm turning
into a frog.

You're just playing
too much croquet.

Knock Knock!
Who's there?
Eamon.
Eamon who?
Eamon a good mood today, thank you!

Knock Knock!
Who's there?
Sherwood.
Sherwood who?
Sherwood like to meet you!

Knock Knock!
Who's there?
Boliva.
Boliva who?
Boliva me I know what I'm talking about!

Knock Knock!
Who's there?
Zookeeper.
Zookeeper who?
Zookeeper away from him!

Knock Knock!
Who's there?
Ester.
Ester who?
Ester anything I can do for you?

Knock Knock!
Who's there?
Eve.
Eve who?
Eve ho me hearties!

Knock Knock!
Who's there?
Watson.
Watson who?
Watson television?

Knock Knock!
Who's there?
Abbott.
Abbott who?
Abbott time you opened the door!

Knock Knock!
Who's there?
Zizi.
Zizi who?
Zizi when you know how!

Knock Knock!
Who's there?
Tennessee.
Tennessee who?
Tennessee you later!

Knock Knock!
Who's there?
Julia.
Julia who?
Julia want some cookies?

Knock Knock!
Who's there?
Buddha.
Buddha who?
Buddha this slice of bread for me!

Knock Knock!
Who's there?
Reed.
Reed who?
Reed-turn to sender, address unknown!

Knock Knock!
Who's there?
Weasel.
Weasel who?
Weasel while you work!

Knock Knock!
Who's there?
Daisy.
Daisy who?
Daisy said you were in but I don't believe them!

Knock Knock!
Who's there?
Lisa.
Lisa who?
Lisa you can do is let me in!

Doctor, doctor, I dream there are monsters under my bed. What can I do?

Saw the legs off your bed.

Doctor, doctor, I feel like a packet of biscuits.

Oh, you're crackers.

Doctor, doctor, I'm becoming invisible.

Yes, I can see you're not all there.

Doctor, doctor, my little
boy has just swallowed a
roll of film.

Let's hope nothing
develops.

Doctor, doctor, when I press
with my finger here ... it hurts,
and here ... it hurts, and here
and here. What do you think is
wrong with me?

You have a broken finger!

Knock Knock!
Who's there?
Jamie.
Jamie who?
Jamie'n you don't recognise my voice?

Knock Knock!
Who's there?
Catsup.
Catsup who?
Catsup a tree and she won't come down!

Knock Knock!
Who's there?
Cash.
Cash who?
I knew you were nuts!

Knock Knock!
Who's there?
Closure.
Closure who?
Closure mouth when you're eating!

Knock Knock!
Who's there?
Len.
Len who?
Len me a fiver!

Knock Knock!
Who's there?
L.A.
L.A. who?
L.A. down for a snooze and slept all afternoon!

Knock Knock!
Who's there?
Mind.
Mind who?
Mind your own business!

Knock Knock!
Who's there?
Dishwasher.
Dishwasher who?
Dishwasher way I talked before I got my new teeth!

Knock Knock!
Who's there?
Mark.
Mark who?
Mark your calendar, my birthday's soon!

Knock Knock!
Who's there?
Jimmy.
Jimmy who?
Jimmy some cake I'm starving!

Knock Knock!
Who's there?
Chuck.
Chuck who?
Chuck-olate bunny!

Knock Knock!
Who's there?
Witch.
Witch who?
Witch you stop asking and open the door?

74

Knock Knock!
Who's there?
Howard.
Howard who?
**Howard you like
to go out today?**

Knock Knock!
Who's there?
Ivan.
Ivan who?
Ivan headache!

Knock Knock!
Who's there?
Button.
Button who?
**Button in is
not polite!**

Knock Knock!
Who's there?
Eustace.
Eustace who?
**Come Eustace
you are!**

Doctor, doctor,
I snore so loudly I keep
myself awake.

Sleep in another room then.

Doctor, doctor, I've a
split personality.

Well, you'd better both
sit down then.

Doctor, doctor, my son
has swallowed my pen.
What should I do?

Use a pencil until
I get there.

Doctor: You seem to be in excellent health. Your pulse is as regular as clockwork.

Patient: That's because you've got your hand on my watch.

Doctor, doctor, I think I'm suffering from déjà vu!

Didn't I see you yesterday?

What do you call a flea that lives in an idiot's ear?

A space invader!

What do you get if you cross a rabbit and a flea?

Bugs Bunny!

How do you start an insect race?

One, two, flea – go!

Where do fleas live?

Fleadelphia!

What is the
difference between
a flea and a wolf?

One prowls on the
hairy and the other
howls on the prairie!

How do you find
where a flea has
bitten you?

Start from scratch!

What do you
call a Russian flea?

A Moscow-ito!

Knock Knock!
Who's there?
Duck.
Duck who?
Just duck!
They're throwing
things at us!

Knock Knock!
Who's there?
Hoo.
Hoo who?
Is there an owl
in here?

Knock Knock!
Who's there?
Lion.
Lion who?
Lion on your
doorstep, open up!

Knock Knock!
Who's there?
Argue.
Argue who?
Argue going to
let me in or not?

Knock Knock!
Who's there?
Mae.
Mae who?
Mae be I'll tell you and Mae be I won't!

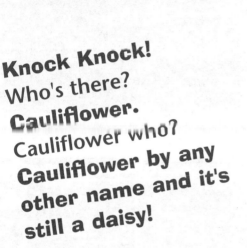

Knock Knock!
Who's there?
Cauliflower.
Cauliflower who?
Cauliflower by any other name and it's still a daisy!

Knock Knock!
Who's there?
Alec.
Alec who?
Alec-tricity. Isn't that a shock!

Knock Knock!
Who's there?
Bacon.
Bacon who?
Bacon a cake for your birthday!

Doctor, doctor, I've had tummy ache since I ate three crabs yesterday.

Did they smell bad when you took them out of their shells?

What do you mean, 'took them out of their shells'?

Doctor, doctor, I keep thinking I'm a dog.

Sit on the couch and we will talk about it.

But I'm not allowed up on the couch!

Doctor, doctor, I think
I need glasses.

You certainly do, Sir. This
is a fish and chip shop.

Doctor, doctor, I've got wind.
Can you give me something?

Yes — here's a kite.

Doctor, doctor, how
do I stop my nose
from running?

Stick your foot out
and trip it up.

What did the dog do with the history professor?

They got together and talked over old times.

What did the dog get when he multiplied 497 by 684?

The wrong answer.

What did the dog say to the candle?

'Are you going out tonight?'

What did the dog say to the pig?

'You are just a bore.'

What did the dog say when he chased his tail?

'This is the end.'

What did the dog take when he was run down?

The licence number of the car that hit him.

What did the dog tell his owner when he saw the dog-catcher coming?

Nothing. Dogs don't talk.

What does a dog become after it is six years old?

Seven years old.

What do
bees chew?

Bumble gum!

What does a cat
go to sleep on?

A caterpillow!

Why are As like
flowers?

Because Bs come
after them!

What does a
caterpillar do on
New Year's Day?

Turns over a
new leaf!

What is the definition of a caterpillar?

A worm in a fur coat!

What has stripes and pulls a tractor?

A caterpillar tractor!

What is worse than a giraffe with a sore throat?

A centipede with chilblains!

What has 50 legs but can't walk?

Half a centipede!

Doctor, doctor, my baby's swallowed a bullet.

Well don't point him at anyone until I get there.

Doctor, doctor, I've just swallowed a pen.

Well sit down and write your name!

Doctor, doctor, I feel like a serial.

I'll tell you your problem next week.

Doctor, doctor, I keep thinking I'm a frog.

What's wrong with that?

I think I'm going to croak.

Doctor, doctor, how can I cure my sleepwalking?

Sprinkle drawing pins on your bedroom floor.

Doctor, doctor, am I a mosquito?

That's your problem, sucker.

What do angry spiders do?

They go up the wall.

Two fleas were running across the top of a cereal packet.

'Why are we running so fast?' asked one.

'Because it says "tear along the dotted line"!'

What is the most faithful insect?

A flea – once they find someone they like, they stick to them!

What do you call a cheerful flea?

A hop-timist!

What did
the romantic
flea say?

'I love you aw-flea!'

Why is a polar bear
a cheap pet?

It lives
on ice!

How do you keep
flies out of the
kitchen?

Put a pile of manure
in the living room!

What is the
difference between
a fly and a bird?

A bird can fly but
a fly can't bird!

Knock Knock!
Who's there?
Norway.
Norway who?
Norway will I leave until you open this door!

Knock Knock!
Who's there?
Ina.
Ina who?
Ina minute I'm going to knock this door down!

Knock Knock!
Who's there?
Banana.
Banana who?
Banana split so ice creamed!

Knock Knock!
Who's there?
Robin.
Robin who?
Robin the bank!

Knock Knock!
Who's there?
Alaska.
Alaska who?
Alaska my friend the question!

Knock Knock!
Who's there?
Pudding.
Pudding who?
Pudding your shoes on before your trousers is stupid!

Knock Knock!
Who's there?
Steve.
Steve who?
Steve upper lip!

Knock Knock!
Who's there?
Europe.
Europe who?
Europe'ning the door too slowly! Come on!

Doctor, doctor, my sister thinks she's a lift.

Well tell her to come in.

I can't — she doesn't stop at this floor.

Doctor, doctor, people keep throwing me into bins.

Don't talk rubbish.

Doctor, doctor, I keep hearing a ringing sound.

Try answering the phone.

Doctor, doctor, I keep seeing funny spots before my eyes.

Have you seen a doctor before?

No, just funny spots.

Doctor, doctor, I feel like a £50 note.

Go to the shops — the change will do you good.

Doctor, doctor, I have this feeling that I'm invisible.

Did I hear a voice?

Knock Knock!
Who's there?
Candy.
Candy who?
Candy cow jump over the moon?

Knock Knock!
Who's there?
Cheese.
Cheese who?
Cheese to meet you!

Knock Knock!
Who's there?
Iguana.
Iguana who?
Iguana hold your hand!

Knock Knock!
Who's there?
Gary.
Gary who?
Gary on typing!

Knock Knock!
Who's there?
Aida.
Aida who?
Aida lot of sweets and now my tummy aches!

Knock Knock!
Who's there?
Kay.
Kay who?
K, L, M, N, O, P, Q, R, S, T, U, V, W, X, Y, Z!

Knock Knock!
Who's there?
I don't know.
I don't know who?
I don't know. Why don't you believe me?

Knock Knock!
Who's there?
Adair.
Adair who?
Adair hair but now I'm bald.

What did the angry man sing when he found his slippers chewed up by the new puppy?

'I must throw that doggie out the window!'

Why do dogs wag their tails?

Because no one else will do it for them!

What happened to the dog that ate nothing but garlic?

His bark was much worse than his bite!

Why do dogs bury bones in the ground?

Because you can't bury them in trees!

98

What happened when the dog went to the flea circus?

He stole the show!

How do you know if you have a stupid dog?

It chases parked cars!

What do you get if you cross a dog with Concorde?

A jet setter!

Why did the dog wear white sneakers?

Because his boots were at the menders!

Doctor, doctor, will I be able to swim after this operation? Yes.

Great, I never could before.

Doctor, doctor, I keep eating dog food.

I'm a doctor, not a vet.

Doctor, doctor, I keep thinking I'm a drill.

How boring for you.

Doctor, doctor — I've lost
my ears!

Listen, this is what
I'm going to do.

Doctor, doctor, I
think I've broken
my neck.

Don't worry — keep
your chin up.

Doctor, doctor, I've got
delayed vision.

I'll see you in a minute, then.

Knock Knock!
Who's there?
Blue.
Blue who?
Blue away with the wind!

Knock Knock!
Who's there?
Keanu.
Keanu who?
Keanu let me in, it's cold out here!

Knock Knock!
Who's there?
Termite.
Termite who?
Termite's the night!

Knock Knock!
Who's there?
Ivan.
Ivan who?
**Ivan new hat.
Do you like it?**

Knock Knock!
Who's there?
Yule.
Yule who.
Yule never know!

Knock Knock!
Who's there?
Samuel.
Samuel who?
Samuel be famous one day!

Knock Knock!
Who's there?
Rhoda.
Rhoda who?
Row row rhoda boat ...

Knock Knock!
Who's there?
Abba.
Abba who?
Abba-out turn! Quick march!

What did the dog use to make his kite?

Flypaper.

What dog can jump higher than a tree?

Any dog can jump higher than a tree. Trees don't jump.

What eats dog food, lives in a doghouse and is very dangerous?

A dog with a machine gun.

What pill would you give to an elephant that can't sleep?

Trunquilizers!

What do you call a three-legged donkey?

A wonkey.

What's the difference between an elephant and a gooseberry?

A gooseberry is green!

A boy with an elephant on his head went to see a doctor. The doctor said, 'You know, you really need help.'

'Yes I do,' said the elephant, 'get this kid off my foot!'

Why do elephants have trunks?

Because they would look silly carrying suitcases!

Doctor, doctor, I've just swallowed my mouth organ.

Well look on the bright side, at least you weren't playing a grand piano.

Doctor, doctor, I feel like an untidy nun.

Well, that's a dirty habit.

Doctor, doctor, I feel like a chair thief.

Please take a seat, then.

Doctor, doctor, is there anything wrong with my heart?

After a thorough examination I can say it will last as long as you do.

Doctor, doctor, can you recommend anything for flat feet?

How about a foot pump?

Doctor, doctor, I think I'm a canary.

Don't worry — it's tweetable.

Knock Knock!
Who's there?
Uganda.
Uganda who?
Uganda get away with this!

Knock Knock!
Who's there?
Leaf.
Leaf who?
Leaf me alone!

Knock Knock!
Who's there?
You.
You who?
You who, is anybody in?

Knock Knock!
Who's there?
Quacker.
Quacker who?
Quacker another bad joke and I'm leaving!

Knock Knock!
Who's there?
Farmer.
Farmer who?
Farmer birthday I'm getting a new bike!

Knock Knock!
Who's there?
Rabbit.
Rabbit who?
Rabbit up carefully, it's a present!

Knock Knock!
Who's there?
Sherlock.
Sherlock who?
Sherlock your back door, someone will break in!

Knock Knock!
Who's there?
Norma Lee.
Norma Lee who?
Norma Lee I have my key!

What kind of meat do you give a stupid dog?

Chump chops!

What sort of clothes does a pet dog wear?

A petticoat!

What do you get if you cross a sheepdog with a rose?

A collie-flower!

Why did the dachshund bite the woman's ankle?

Because he was short and couldn't reach any higher!

Why did the
snowman call his
dog Frost?

Because
frost bites!

Why did the poor dog
chase his own tail?

He was trying to make
both ends meet!

Where does a rottweiler
sit in the cinema?

Anywhere it wants to!

What does a lion
brush his mane with?

A catacomb!

Doctor, doctor, I keep eating little bits of metal.

That sounds like a staple diet.

Doctor, doctor, I feel like a car.

Park yourself over there a moment.

Doctor, doctor, I think I'm a jelly baby.

SHUT UP!

Ok, ok — there's no need to bite my head off.

Doctor, doctor, I'm not well — can you give me something to make me better?

Take two teaspoons of this after every meal.

But, doctor, I've only got one teaspoon.

Doctor, doctor, how can I avoid falling hair?

Move out of the way.

Doctor, doctor, what's the best cure for dandruff?

Baldness.

Knock Knock!
Who's there?
Camilla.
Camilla who?
Camilla minute!

Knock Knock!
Who's there?
A Fred.
A Fred who?
Whose a Fred of the Big, Bad Wolf?

Knock Knock!
Who's there?
Yolanda.
Yolanda who?
Yolanda some money?

Knock Knock!
Who's there?
Madrid.
Madrid who?
Madrid you wash my jeans?

Knock Knock!
Who's there?
Teddy.
Teddy who?
**Teddy is the beginning
of the rest of your life!**

Knock Knock!
Who's there?
Bless.
Bless who?
I didn't sneeze!

Knock Knock!
Who's there?
Alex.
Alex who?
Alex plain later!

Knock Knock!
Who's there?
Almond.
Almond who?
**Almond the side
of the law!**

What do polar bears have for lunch?

Ice burgers.

What goes hum-choo, hum-choo?

A bee with a cold.

What's a bee-line?

The shortest distance between two buzz-stops!

What is the difference between an elephant and a flea?

An elephant can have fleas but a flea can't have elephants!

Why do bees hum?

Because they've forgotten the words!

Why did the elephant paint his toenails rod?

So he could hide in the cherry tree!

What do you call an elephant that flies?

A jumbo jet!

How do you know when there is an elephant under your bed?

When your nose touches the ceiling!

A man walked into the doctor's office with a huge frog on his head.

The doctor asked, 'What seems to be the problem?'

The frog said, 'I have this huge wart on my bottom that I can't get rid of.'

What did the surgeon say when he severed an artery?

Aorta know better.

Doctor, doctor, how long can a man live without a brain?

I don't know. How old are you?

Doctor, doctor, a dog has just bitten my leg.

Did you put anything on it?

No, he liked it just the way it was.

Doctor, doctor, I feel like a toilet.

You do look a little flushed.

What bee is good for your health?

Vitamin bee!

What is black and yellow and buzzes along at 30,000 feet?

A bee in an aeroplane!

What does a bee say before it stings you?

'This is going to hurt me a lot more than it hurts you!'

Who are the cleverest bees?

Spelling bees!

Why did the queen bee kick out all of the other bees?

Because they kept droning on and on!

How many bees do you need in a bee choir?

A humdred!

What pillar doesn't need holding up?

A caterpillar!

What kind of bee can keep an aeroplane dry?

An aero-drone!

Knock Knock!
Who's there?
Vaughn.
Vaughn who?
Vaughn day my prince will come!

Knock Knock!
Who's there?
Violet.
Violet who?
Violet the cat out of the bag?

Knock Knock!
Who's there?
Truffle.
Truffle who?
Truffle with you is that you're too shy!

Knock Knock!
Who's there?
Nadia.
Nadia who?
Just Nadia head if you understand!

Knock Knock!
Who's there?
Imogen.
Imogen who?
Imogen life without chocolate!

Knock Knock!
Who's there?
Wanda.
Wanda who?
Wanda get some cake?

Knock Knock!
Who's there?
Lionel.
Lionel who?
Lionel get you nowhere, tell the truth!

Knock Knock!
Who's there?
Bach.
Bach who?
Bach to work you slackers!

Doctor, doctor, I just swallowed a worm.

Let me give you something for it.

No thanks — I'll just let it starve.

Doctor, doctor, I think I'm a goat.

How long have you thought this?

Since I was a kid.

Doctor, doctor, do you have something for my kidneys?

How about some bacon?

Doctor, doctor,
I feel like a
window.

Do you have
a pane?

Doctor: How are
those pills I
prescribed for your
failing memory
working?

Patient: What pills?

Patient: This
is the first operation
I've ever had.

Doctor: Don't worry,
this is the first
operation I've done.

Knock Knock!
Who's there?
Ray.
Ray who?
Ray-ning cats
and dogs!

Knock Knock!
Who's there?
Ear.
Ear who?
Ear you are,
I've been looking
for you!

Knock Knock!
Who's there?
Humphrey.
Humphrey who?
Hum three notes and
I'll name that tune!

Knock Knock!
Who's there?
Peek Ash.
Peek Ash who?
Pikachu, I
choose you!

126

Knock Knock!
Who's there?
Avenue.
Avenue who?
Avenue heard this joke before?

Knock Knock!
Who's there?
Window.
Window who?
Window I get my dinner?

Knock Knock!
Who's there?
Senior.
Senior who?
Senior so nosey, I'm not going to tell you!

Knock Knock!
Who's there?
Disease.
Disease who?
Disease trousers fit you?

What did the naughty spider do?

He told a web of lies.

Why are spiders good swimmers?

They have webbed feet!

What do you get if you cross a skunk with a teddy bear?

Winnie-the-Pooh.

What do you call a bee who's had a spell put on him?

Bee-witched!

Can bees fly
in the rain?

Not without
their little yellow
jackets!

What buzzes,
is black and yellow
and goes along
the bottom
of the sea?

A bee in a
submarine!

What's a lion's
favourite food?

Baked beings!

What would happen
if tarantulas were as
big as horses?

If one bit you, you
could ride it to
hospital!

Why do doctors and nurses wear masks?

So if they make a mistake, you won't know who did it.

Dentist: Have your teeth ever been checked?

Patient: No, they've always been white.

Doctor: Nurse, did you take the patient's temperature?

Nurse: Why? Is it missing?

Why did the biscuit
go to the doctor?

Because it was
feeling crummy.

Doctor, doctor,
I'm worried about
my figure.

You'll just have
to diet.

What colour?

How does
an apple a day
keep the doctor
away?

You have to aim
it correctly.

Doctor, doctor,
I've only got 59
seconds to live!

Just a minute
please.

Knock Knock!
Who's there?
Iam.
Iam who?
Sorry I don't know who you are!

Knock Knock!
Who's there?
Letter.
Letter who?
Letter keep knocking!

Knock Knock!
Who's there?
Alpaca.
Alpaca who?
Alpaca lunch, let's go for a picnic!

Knock Knock!
Who's there?
Tom Sawyer.
Tom Sawyer who?
Tom sawyer underwear!

Knock Knock!
Who's there?
Utah.
Utah who?
You talking to me?

Knock Knock!
Who's there?
Oscar.
Oscar who?
Oscar stupid question, you get a stupid answer!

Knock Knock!
Who's there?
Sherwood.
Sherwood who?
Sure would like you to open the door!

Knock Knock!
Who's there?
Mike.
Mike who?
My cup is empty. Can I have a refill?

Knock Knock!
Who's there?
Wanda.
Wanda who?
Wanda where I put my car keys?

Knock Knock!
Who's there?
Jamaica.
Jamaica who?
Jamaica good grade on the test?

Knock Knock!
Who's there?
Carrot.
Carrot who?
Do you carrot all about me?

Knock Knock!
Who's there?
Wooden.
Wooden who?
Wooden you like to know!

134

Knock Knock!
Who's there?
Stan.
Stan who?
Stan back, I think I'm going to sneeze!

Knock Knock!
Who's there?
Conrad.
Conrad who?
Conradulations, I used your joke!

Knock Knock!
Who's there?
Distressing.
Distressing who?
Distressing has too much vinegar!

Knock Knock!
Who's there?
Ewe.
Ewe who?
Who me? What do you want?

Doctor, doctor, I think I'm a dog.

You're probably imagining it, but until we're sure, get off the couch.

Why is a cold germ stronger than a man?

Because it can bring a man to his sneeze.

Doctor, doctor, how do I stop a head cold reaching my chest?

Tie a knot in your neck.

Doctor, doctor,
I think I'm a bird.

Perch yourself there
and I'll tweet you in
a minute.

Doctor, doctor,
I keep seeing
spots before
my eyes.

You should have
them checked.

Doctor, doctor,
I feel half dead.

Don't worry — I'll bury you
up to your waist.

Why did the fly fly?
Because the spider spied her.

What has six legs, bites and talks in code?

A morse-quito!

What's pretty, delicate and carries a sub-machine-gun?

A killer butterfly!

How do you make a butter-fly?

Flick it out of the butter dish with a knife!

What insect lives on nothing?

A moth, because it eats holes.

What do insects learn at school?

Mothmatics!

What do you get if you cross a firefly and a moth?

An insect who can find its way around a dark wardrobe!

How do stones stop moths eating your clothes?

Because rolling stones gather no moths!

Knock Knock!
Who's there?
Italian.
Italian who?
Italian you for the last time, open the door!

Knock Knock!
Who's there?
Justin.
Justin who?
Justin the noighbourhood, thought I'd oomn by!

Knock Knock!
Who's there?
Your mum.
Your mum who?
You don't know who your mum is?

Knock Knock!
Who's there?
Sarah.
Sarah who?
Sarah reason you're not laughing?

Knock Knock!
Who's there?
Howard.
Howard who?
Howard your maths test go today?

Knock Knock!
Who's there?
Claire.
Claire who?
Claire the way, I'm coming in!

Knock Knock!
Who's there?
General Lee.
General Lee who?
General Lee I do not tell jokes!

Knock Knock!
Who's there?
House.
House who?
House it going?

Doctor: What have you done for your cold?

Patient: Nothing.

Doctor: Why not?

Patient: Well, it hasn't done anything for me.

Doctor, doctor, I think I'm a yo-yo.

Sit down, stand up, sit down, stand up.

What do you get if you cross a cow with a surgeon?

Cow-operation.

Doctor, doctor, my brother thinks he's a chicken!

Why didn't you bring him here?

We needed the eggs.

Why did the orange go to the doctor?

It wasn't peeling very well.

Doctor, doctor, I feel as sick as a dog.

You'd better see a vet.

Which illness do airline pilots get?

Flu.

Knock Knock!
Who's there?
Colleen.
Colleen who?
Colleen up your room – it's a mess!

Knock Knock!
Who's there?
Kip.
Kip who?
Kip your hands off me!

Knock Knock!
Who's there?
Emma.
Emma who?
Emma cracking you up?

Knock Knock!
Who's there?
Vida.
Vida who?
Vida you talk like that?

Knock Knock!
Who's there?
Rufus.
Rufus who?
Your rufus on fire!

Knock Knock!
Who's there?
Warren.
Warren who?
Warren peace is a famous Russian novel!

Knock Knock!
Who's there?
Hoffman.
Hoffman who?
I'll Hoffman, I'll puff, and I'll blow your house down!

Knock Knock!
Who's there?
Luke.
Luke who?
Luke out! Here comes another knock knock joke!

Knock Knock!
Who's there?
Linnekar.
Linnekar who?
Linnekars in a big traffic jam!

Knock Knock!
Who's there?
Champ.
Champ who?
Champ poo your hair, It's dirty!

Knock Knock!
Who's there?
I Love.
I Love who?
I don't know, who do you love?

Knock Knock!
Who's there?
Holdon.
Holdon who?
Holdon I'll go and see!

146

Knock Knock!
Who's there?
Anna.
Anna who?
Anna body know some more jokes?

Knock Knock!
Who's there?
Dewey.
Dewey who?
Dewey have to listen to all this knocking?

Knock Knock!
Who's there?
Easter.
Easter who?
Easter bunny!

Knock Knock!
Who's there?
Anna.
Anna who?
Anna nother Easter bunny!

Doctor, doctor,
I feel like a
dumpling.

Don't get yourself
in a stew.

Doctor, doctor,
I feel like duck-doo.

What's a duck-doo?

It goes quack-quack,
of course.

Doctor, doctor,
everything I swallow
comes up.

Here, swallow my
lottery numbers.

148

Patient: What should I do about my broken leg?

Doctor: Limp.

Doctor, doctor, I think I should see a psychiatrist.

You need your head examined.

Doctor, doctor, my nose runs and my feet smell — what's wrong with me?

You were made upside-down.

Knock Knock!
Who's there?
Max.
Max who?
Max no difference!

Knock Knock!
Who's there?
Dishes.
Dishes who?
Dishes me.
Who is this?

Knock Knock!
Who's there?
Ketchup.
Ketchup who?
**Ketchup to me
and I'll tell you!**

Knock Knock!
Who's there?
Madam.
Madam who?
**Madam finger is
stuck in the door!**

Knock Knock!
Who's there?
Daisy.
Daisy who?
**Daisy plays, night
he sleeps!**

Knock Knock!
Who's there?
Doris.
Doris who?
**Doris open,
come on in!**

Knock Knock!
Who's there?
Little old lady.
Little old lady who?
**I didn't know you
could yodel!**

Knock Knock!
Who's there?
Aware.
Aware who?
**Aware oh where
have my little
sheep gone?**

Knock Knock!
Who's there?
Omelette.
Omelette who?
Omelette smarter than I look!

Knock Knock!
Who's there?
Spider.
Spider who?
You tried to hide her, but I spider!

Knock Knock!
Who's there?
Dexter.
Dexter who?
Dexter hall with boughs of holly!

Knock Knock!
Who's there?
Goat.
Goat who?
Goat to the door and find out!

Knock Knock!
Who's there?
Ilona.
Ilona who?
Ilona Ranger!

Knock Knock!
Who's there?
Labrador.
Labrador who?
Labrador is a city, not a person!

Knock Knock!
Who's there?
Arthur.
Arthur who?
Arthur any more at home like you?

Knock Knock!
Who's there?
Warrior.
Warrior who?
Warrior been all my life?

Doctor, doctor, there's something wrong with my stomach.

Zip up your coat and no one will notice.

Doctor, doctor, I'm at death's door.

Don't worry — I'll pull you through.

Which famous saint always had a cold?

Saint Francis of Asneezi.

Doctor, doctor, I think I'm a horse.

I can cure you but it will cost a lot of money.

That's ok — I've just won the Grand National.

Which famous painter always had a cold?

Vincent Van Cough.

Where do sick wasps go?

To the waspital.

Knock Knock!
Who's there?
Avon.
Avon who?
Avon to be alone!

Knock Knock!
Who's there?
Butcher.
Butcher who?
Butcher arms around me!

Knock Knock!
Who's there?
Abyssinia.
Abyssinia who?
Abyssinia soon!

Knock Knock!
Who's there?
Major.
Major who?
Major open the door, didn't I?

Knock Knock!
Who's there?
Manny.
Manny who?
**Manny are called,
but few are chosen!**

Knock Knock!
Who's there?
Donna.
Donna who?
**Donna sit under
the apple tree?**

Knock Knock!
Who's there?
Sony.
Sony who?
Sony a paper moon!

Knock Knock!
Who's there?
Doughnut.
Doughnut who?
**Doughnut ask me
that silly question!**

157

Knock Knock!
Who's there?
Elsie.
Elsie who?
**Elsie you in my
dreams!**

Knock Knock!
Who's there?
Dwayne.
Dwayne who?
**Dwayne the
swimming pool,
it's full of bugs!**

Knock Knock!
Who's there?
Pizza.
Pizza who?
**Pizza on Earth and
goodwill to all men!**

Knock Knock!
Who's there?
Lil.
Lil who?
**Lil things count
the most!**

Knock Knock!
Who's there?
Frank and Stan.
Frank and Stan who?
Frankenstein the monster!

Knock Knock!
Who's there?
Athea.
Athea who?
Athea later alligator!

Knock Knock!
Who's there?
Andy.
Andy who?
Andy that he has to give me all his sweets!

Knock Knock!
Who's there?
Myth.
Myth who?
Myth you too!

Doctor: You have acute appendicitis.

Patient: Thank you — I'm glad you like it.

Doctor, doctor, I feel like the pipe that sticks out of a car.

Yes, you do look exhausted.

Which creature performs underwater operations?

A doctorpus.

160

Patient: The cream you gave me makes my arms smart.

Doctor: Well, rub it on your head then.

Doctor: Go to the window and stick your tongue out.

Patient: What will that tell you?

Doctor: Nothing, I just don't like the lady who lives opposite.

Doctor, doctor, I think I'm a fridge.

Shut your mouth — you're shining your light right in my eyes.

Knock Knock!
Who's there?
Alison.
Alison who?
**Alison to my radio
in the morning!**

Knock Knock!
Who's there?
Kent.
Kent who?
Kent you tell?

Knock Knock!
Who's there?
Sabina.
Sabina who?
**Sabina long time
since I saw you!**

Knock Knock!
Who's there?
Olive.
Olive who?
**Olive here, now
let me in!**

Knock Knock!
Who's there?
Wooden shoe.
Wooden shoe who?
**Wooden shoe like
to know!**

Knock Knock!
Who's there?
Felix.
Felix who?
**Felix my ice cream
again, I'll bash him!**

Knock Knock!
Who's there?
Snow.
Snow who?
**Snow use, I've
forgotten my
name again!**

Knock Knock!
Who's there?
Canoe.
Canoe who?
**Canoe help me with my
homework, please?**

163

Knock Knock!
Who's there?
Alba.
Alba who?
**Alba in the kitchen
if you need me!**

Knock Knock!
Who's there?
Frank.
Frank who?
**Frank you for
being my friend!**

Knock Knock!
Who's there?
Aladdin.
Aladdin who?
**Aladdin the street
wants a word with you!**

Knock Knock!
Who's there?
Interrupting cow.
Interrupti-
Mooooooo!

164

Knock Knock!
Who's there?
Alex.
Alex who?
Alex the questions around here!

Knock Knock!
Who's there?
Carl.
Carl who?
Carl get you there quicker than walking!

Knock Knock!
Who's there?
De Niro.
De Niro who?
De Niro I am to you the more I like you!

Knock Knock!
Who's there?
Nuisance.
Nuisance who?
What's nuisance yesterday?

Doctor, doctor, I feel like a frog that's lost its voice.

It could be that you have a man in your throat.

Doctor, doctor, I feel like a goat.

Well now, how are the kids?

Why is being in hospital funny?

Because the surgeon has you in stitches.

Doctor, doctor, I forgot to shake the bottle before I took my medicine.

That's ok — just jump up and down now.

Doctor, doctor, I've lost my sense of touch.

So, you're not feeling very well ...

Doctor, doctor, I think I'm an ant.

Stop bugging me.

Knock Knock!
Who's there?
Haiti.
Haiti who?
Haiti see good food go to waste!

Knock Knock!
Who's there?
Tyson.
Tyson who?
Tyson of this on for size!

Knock Knock!
Who's there?
India.
India who?
India night time I go to sleep!

Knock Knock!
Who's there?
Andy.
Andy who?
Andy bit me again!

Knock Knock!
Who's there?
Broccoli.
Broccoli who?
Broccoli doesn't have a second name!

Knock Knock!
Who's there?
Apple.
Apple who?
Apple your hair if you don't let me in!

Knock Knock!
Who's there?
Cheese.
Cheese who?
Cheese a good girl!

Knock Knock!
Who's there?
Berlin.
Berlin who?
Berlin the water to cook an egg!

Knock Knock!
Who's there?
Insect.
Insect who?
Insect your name here!

Knock Knock!
Who's there?
Pickle.
Pickle who?
Oh, that's my favourite instrument!

Knock Knock!
Who's there?
Read.
Read who?
Read between the lines!

Knock Knock!
Who's there?
Ice cream soda.
Ice cream soda who?
Ice cream soda whole world knows what a nut you are!

170

Knock Knock!
Who's there?
A herd.
A herd who?
A herd you were home so I came over!

Knock Knock!
Who's there?
No one.
No one who?
NO ONE!

Knock Knock!
Who's there?
Ivor.
Ivor who?
Ivor you let me in or I climb through the window!

Knock Knock!
Who's there?
Officer O'Brian.
Officer O'Brian who?
Officer O'Brian from the police station!

Doctor, doctor, I've got a pain in my leg.

I think it's down to old age.

But the other one is the same age and it feels fine.

Doctor, doctor, I feel like an apple.

Don't worry, I won't pick you.

Doctor, doctor, I think I'm a fly.

Come down from the ceiling and I'll deal with you.

Doctor: I'm sorry but you only have three minutes to live.

Patient: Is there nothing you can do for me?

Doctor: I could boil you an egg.

Doctor, doctor, I feel like an onion.

Don't get in a pickle.

Doctor, doctor, I feel like a sore pig.

I've got some oinkment for that.

Knock Knock!
Who's there?
Norman.
Norman who?
Norman invasion 1066!

Knock Knock!
Who's there?
Maggot?
Maggot who?
Maggot me this new shirt today!

Knock Knock!
Who's there?
I've done up.
I've done up who?
Ha Ha Ha Ha!

Knock Knock!
Who's there?
Dismay.
Dismay who?
Dismay be a joke but it's not funny!

Knock Knock!
Who's there?
July.
July who?
July or you tell the truth?

Knock Knock!
Who's there?
Amanda.
Amanda who?
Amanda doctor's orders at the moment!

Knock Knock!
Who's there?
Ewan.
Ewan who?
Ewan me are supposed to go out today!

Knock Knock!
Who's there?
Ida.
Ida who?
Ida awful day today!

Knock Knock!
Who's there?
Theo.
Theo who?
The cinema is showing a good film tonight. Do you want to go?

Knock Knock!
Who's there?
Justin.
Justin who?
Justin time I found you!

Knock Knook!
Who's there?
Sandy.
Sandy who?
Sandy shore!

Knock Knock!
Who's there?
Mabel.
Mabel who?
Mabel isn't working either!

Knock Knock!
Who's there?
Kermit.
Kermit who?
**Kermit a crime
and you go to jail!**

Knock Knock!
Who's there?
Mary.
Mary who?
**Mary Christmas
everyone!**

Knock Knock!
Who's there?
Lydia.
Lydia who?
**Lydia dustbin
is loose!**

Knock Knock!
Who's there?
Norma.
Norma who?
**Normally the butler
opens the door!**

Doctor, doctor, I've been stung by a bee.

I'll give you some cream to put on it.

Don't be silly — it'll be miles away by now.

Doctor, doctor, I feel like a wizard.

I think you should have a spell in bed.

Doctor, doctor, I feel like a horse with a cold.

Here, try this cough stirrup.

Doctor: In my opinion, you have three days to live. Is there anyone you would like to see?

Patient: Yes, another doctor.

Doctor, doctor, I keep seeing frogs in front of my eyes.

It's just a hop-tical illusion.

Patient: What's the best way to prevent diseases caused by biting insects?

Doctor: Don't bite any.

Knock Knock!
Who's there?
Amanda.
Amanda who?
Amanda the table!

Knock Knock!
Who's there?
Innuendo.
Innuendo who?
Innuendo the dinner you get dessert!

Knock Knock!
Who's there?
Pear.
Pear who?
Pear of shoes!

Knock Knock!
Who's there?
Wicked.
Wicked who?
Wicked make music together!

Knock Knock!
Who's there?
Bella.
Bella who?
Bella the ball!

Knock Knock!
Who's there?
Perry.
Perry who?
**Perry well,
thank you!**

Knock Knock!
Who's there?
Micky.
Micky who?
**Micky won't fit in
the lock – that's
why I'm knocking!**

Knock Knock!
Who's there?
Dummy.
Dummy who?
**Dummy a favour
and let me in!**

What is the difference between Father Christmas and a warm dog?

Father Christmas wears a whole suit, a dog just pants!

How can you get a set of teeth put in for free?

Hit a lion!

When is the most likely time that a stray dog will walk into your house?

When the door is open!

What do you get if you cross a dog and a cheetah?

A dog that chases cars – and catches them!

182

What happens when it rains cats and dogs?

You can step in a poodle!

What kind of dog sounds like you can eat it?

A sausage dog!

What goes 99-clonk, 99-clonk, 99-clonk?

A centipede with a wooden leg!

What is worse than an alligator with toothache?

A centipede with athlete's foot!

Doctor, doctor,
I feel like a
bookcase.

Why do you
say that?

I keep talking to
my shelf.

Doctor, doctor,
I feel like an
injured citrus fruit.

Nurse, this man
needs lemon-aid.

Patient: Doctor,
I feel like an apple.

Nurse: Sorry — an
apple a day keeps
the doctor away.

Why did the nurse
tiptoe past the
medicine cabinet?

She didn't want to wake
the sleeping pills.

Doctor, doctor, I'm
feeling run-down.

Try looking both
ways before you
cross the road.

Doctor, doctor, tell me
how I stand.

I don't know — it's a
miracle to me.

What do you get if you cross a centipede and a parrot?

A walkie talkie!

What do you do if your dog eats your pen?

Use a poncil instead!

Why don't dogs make good dancers?

Because they have two left feet!

What do you get if you cross a rottweiler and a hyena?

I don't know, but I'll join in if it laughs!

186

What do dogs
have that no other
animal has?

Puppy dogs!

What do you call a
fake noodle?

An Impasta!

What is a dog's
favourite sport?

Formula One
drooling!

What is a dog's
favourite food?

Anything that is on
your plate!

Knock Knock!
Who's there?
Cat.
Cat who?
Caterpillar!

Knock Knock!
Who's there?
Yula.
Yula who?
Yula apologise for not letting me in sooner!

Knock Knock!
Who's there?
Alec.
Alec who?
Alec Jack, but I don't like you!

Knock Knock!
Who's there?
White.
White who?
White in the middle!

Knock Knock!
Who's there?
Money.
Money who?
Money is stiff, I hurt it playing football!

Knock Knock!
Who's there?
Major.
Major who?
Major answer, didn't I!

Knock Knock!
Who's there?
CDs.
CDs who?
CDs fingers? They're freezing! Let me in!

Knock Knock!
Who's there?
Ivan.
Ivan who?
Ivan infectious disease!

Patient: Why are you writing on my toes?

Doctor: I'm adding a footnote.

Doctor, doctor, I think I've got chicken pox.

That's a rash thing to say.

Doctor, doctor, I feel like a pogo stick.

Try this medicine — it'll put a spring in your step.

Nurse: How's the boy who swallowed the £1 coin?

Doctor: No change yet I'm afraid.

Doctor, doctor, I feel like an old sock.

Well I'll be darned.

Doctor, doctor, I can't stop shoplifting.

I'll give you something to take for that.

Knock Knock!
Who's there?
Who stole?
Who stole who?
Who stole what, and I'll tell you if you let me!

Knock Knock!
Who's there?
Judo.
Judo who?
What, Judo know?

Knock Knock!
Who's there?
Imago.
Imago who?
Imago ahead and tell you!

Knock Knock!
Who's there?
Owl.
Owl who?
Owl you know unless you open the door?

Knock Knock!
Who's there?
Jack.
Jack who?
**Jack be nimble,
Jack be quick!**

Knock Knock!
Who's there?
Kook.
Kook who?
**Do you know, you
have a real future
in Swiss clocks!**

Knock Knock!
Who's there?
Archibald.
Archibald who?
**Archibald on top
of your head!**

Knock Knock!
Who's there?
Paul Aidy.
Paul Aidy who?
**Paul Aidy, she
tripped and fell over!**

Knock Knock!
Who's there?
Tim.
Tim who?
Timber!

Knock Knock!
Who's there?
Cockadoodle.
Cockadoodle who?
No! Cockadoodle doo!

Knock Knock!
Who's there?
Tail.
Tail who?
Tail all your friends this joke!

Knock Knock!
Who's there?
William.
William who?
William mind your own business!

Knock Knock!
Who's there?
House.
House who?
House soon do you want to hear this joke?

Knock Knock!
Who's there?
Otto.
Otto who?
Otto know I can't remember!

Knock Knock!
Who's there?
Erma.
Erma who?
Erma little teapot, short and stout!

Doctor, doctor, I feel like a symphony.

I must make some notes about your case.

Doctor, doctor, I feel like a cricket ball.

Howzat?

Doctor, doctor, I swallowed a clock.

Don't alarm yourself.

Doctor: I'm afraid you have rabies.

Patient: Quick! Give me a pen and paper.

Doctor: There's no need to write your will ...

Patient: I'm not, I'm making a list of people to bite.

Doctor, doctor, I feel like a glove.

I think you need a hand.

Doctor, doctor, I think I'm a carrot.

Calm down or you'll get yourself in a stew.

Knock Knock!
Who's there?
Vet.
Vet who?
Vet kind of door is this without a bell?

Knock Knock!
Who's there?
Knock Knock!
Who's there?
Knock Knock!
(Repeat endlessly.)

Knock Knock!
Who's there?
Me.
Me who?
Don't you know who you are yet?

Knock Knock!
Who's there?
What.
What who?
What are you so confused about?

198

Knock Knock!
Who's there?
Huron.
Huron who?
Huron time for once!

Knock Knock!
Who's there?
Sombrero.
Sombrero who?
**Sombrero-ver
the rainbow!**

Knock Knock!
Who's there?
Desil.
Desil who?
**Desil make you
laugh if you're
not too smart!**

Knock Knock!
Who's there?
Cook.
Cook who?
**Hey! Who are you
calling cookoo?**

Knock Knock!
Who's there?
Kenzie.
Kenzie who?
Kenzie it's raining outside?

Knock Knock!
Who's there?
Carl.
Carl who?
Carl'l get you there faster than a bike!

Knock Knock!
Who's there?
Bequick.
Bequick who?
Bequick, your pants are on fire!

Knock Knock!
Who's there?
Adelia.
Adelia who?
Adelia the cards, let's play snap!

Knock Knock!
Who's there?
Diploma.
Diploma who?
Diploma will be here in the morning!

Knock Knock!
Who's there?
Turnip.
Turnip who?
Turnip the music, I love this song!

Knock Knock!
Who's there?
Disguise.
Disguise who?
Disguise the limit!

Knock Knock!
Who's there?
Irish.
Irish who?
Irish I had a million pounds!

Doctor, doctor,
I think I'm a
Christmas cake.

What's got into you?

Flour, butter, cherries,
marzipan ...

Patient: Doctor, I'm
so tired that I don't know
where I am half the time.

Dentist: Open wide, please.

Which kind of fish
performs operations?

A sturgeon.

What happened
to the plastic surgeon
who stood too close
to the fire?

He melted.

Nurse: They say he badly
wanted to be a doctor.

2nd Nurse: He certainly is
a bad doctor.

Doctor, doctor, I feel
like a pencil.

Can we get to the point?

What kind of elephants live in Antarctica?

Cold ones!

How do you fit five elephants into a car?

Two in the front, two in the back and the other in the glove compartment!

How does an elephant get out of a small car?

The same way that he got in!

Why did the elephant cross the road?

Because the chicken was having a day off!

What do you call an elephant at the North Pole?

Lost!

How does a bird with a broken wing manage to land safely?

By sparrowchute!

How do you get an elephant into a matchbox?

Take all the matches out first!

What happened to the elephant who ran away with the circus?

The police made him bring it back!

Knock Knock!
Who's there?
Curt.
Curt who?
Curtsie for the Queen!

Knock Knock!
Who's there?
Alexia.
Alexia who?
Alexia again to open the door!

Knock Knock!
Who's there?
Macon.
Macon who?
Have you got your Macon, it's raining!

Knock Knock!
Who's there?
Dozen.
Dozen who?
Dozen anyone live here anymore?

Knock Knock!
Who's there?
Eureka.
Eureka who?
Eureka of something, it stinks!

Knock Knock!
Who's there?
Kenya.
Kenya who?
Kenya think of anything that's more fun than geography?

Knock Knock!
Who's there?
Lorraine.
Lorraine who?
Lorraine is falling!

Knock Knock!
Who's there?
Kentucky.
Kentucky who?
Kentucky come out to play?

Doctor, doctor,
I feel like a pair
of glasses.

Stop it. You're making
a spectacle of yourself.

Doctor, doctor, this
banana diet isn't
working.

Stop scratching and
come down from
the curtains.

Doctor: Take a deep
breath and say nine
three times.

Patient: Twenty-seven.

Patient: I keep pulling ugly faces.

Doctor: Don't worry, no one will notice.

Doctor, doctor, my husband's broken his leg.

But madam, I'm a doctor of music.

I know — it was the piano that fell on him.

Doctor, doctor, I feel like orange squash.

I'm diluted to meet you.

Knock Knock!
Who's there?
Catch.
Catch who?
Catch me if you can!

Knock Knock!
Who's there?
Eskimo.
Eskimo who?
**Eskimo no
questions, I'll tell
you no lies!**

Knock Knock!
Who's there?
Punch.
Punch who?
**Not me, I just
got here!**

Knock Knock!
Who's there?
Wire.
Wire who?
Wire you asking?

Knock Knock!
Who's there?
Waiter.
Waiter who?
**Waiter minute,
I'll tie my shoelaces!**

Knock Knock!
Who's there?
Opera.
Opera who?
**Opera-tunity. And
you thought
opportunity only
knocked once!**

Knock Knock!
Who's there?
Chimney.
Chimney who?
**Chimney cricket.
Have you seen
Pinocchio?**

Knock Knock!
Who's there?
Aileen Dover.
Aileen Dover who?
Aileen Dover and fell down!

Knock Knock!
Who's there?
Four eggs.
Four eggs who?
Four eggs-ample!

Knock Knock!
Who's there?
I-8.
I-8 who?
I ate lunch already!
Is it time for dinner?

Knock Knock!
Who's there?
Walnuts.
Walnuts who?
Walnuts
around here!

Knock Knock!
Who's there?
One.
One who?
One-derful day,
isn't it?

Knock Knock!
Who's there?
Madam.
Madam who?
**Madam shoe is
stuck in the door!**

Knock Knock!
Who's there?
Abba.
Abba who?
Abba banana!

Knock Knock!
Who's there?
Disk.
Disk who?
**Disk is a recorded
message. Leave
your answer after
the beep!**

Knock Knock!
Who's there?
Island.
Island who?
**Island on your roof
with my parachute!**

Doctor, doctor, I think I'm going deaf.

What is your job?

I'm a fisherman. Why?

I think you need a herring aid.

DOCTOR, DOCTOR, I THINK I'M A HI-FI!

Well, you are definitely a loud speaker.

Doctor: Do your teeth chatter at night?

Patient: I don't know. They're in a glass on the dressing table.

Doctor, doctor, my husband
thinks he's a clothes line.

Bring him to the surgery.

What, and have all my washing
fall on the ground?

Patient: What do
my X-rays show?

Doctor: Well,
both your heads
are all right.

Knock Knock!
Who's there?
Halle.
Halle who?
Hallelujah, you finally opened the door!

Knock Knock!
Who's there?
Tad.
Tad who?
Tad's all folks!

Knock Knock!
Who's there?
Colin.
Colin who?
Colin all doctors! Emergency!

Knock Knock!
Who's there?
Dakota.
Dakota who?
Dakota too long for the arms!

Knock Knock!
Who's there?
Heaven.
Heaven who?
Heaven you heard this joke before?

Knock Knock!
Who's there?
Beets.
Beets who?
Beets me!

Knock Knock!
Who's there?
Roach.
Roach who?
Roach you a letter, didn't you get it?

Knock Knock!
Who's there?
Queen.
Queen who?
Queen as a whistle!

217

Knock Knock!
Who's there?
Oswald.
Oswald who?
Oswald my gum!

Knock Knock!
Who's there?
Tex.
Tex who?
Tex two to tango!

Knock Knock!
Who's there?
Laziness.
Laziness who?
Laziness bed all day, when he should be at school!

Knock Knock!
Who's there?
Denial.
Denial who?
De Nile's a river in Egypt!

Knock Knock!
Who's there?
Rita.
Rita who?
Rita book, you might learn something!

Knock Knock!
Who's there?
Says.
Says who?
Says me!

Knock Knock!
Who's there?
Haden.
Haden who?
Haden seek!

Knock Knock!
Who's there?
Sunday.
Sunday who?
Sunday in the future, you'll let me in!

Doctor: Have you taken the box of pills I gave you?

Patient: Yes, but I think the cardboard disagreed with me.

Doctor: How did you get here?

Patient: I flu.

Doctor: I think your job is making you unhappy. What do you do?

Patient: I write jokes.

220

Patient: My family thinks I'm odd because I like sausages.

Doctor: Really? I like sausages, too.

Patient: You do? Come round to see my collection — I've got hundreds.

Doctor, doctor, will my nostril operation be expensive?

You'll have to pay through the nose.

Doctor, doctor, I feel like a snooker table.

Give me a break.

What kind of
birds do you usually
find locked up?

Jail-birds.

What is the
definition of a robin?

A little bird
that steals.

How many hairs are
in a dog's tail?

None. They are all on
the outside.

If you take your
dog to town,
where should you
leave him?

In a car bark.

If your dog jumped into a swimming pool, what is the first thing he would do?

Get wet.

When is the best time to buy budgies?

When they are going cheap.

What did the dog do when he broke his toe?

He called a tow truck.

What do you call a woodpecker with no beak?

A headbanger!

Knock Knock!
Who's there?
Honeycomb.
Honeycomb who?
**Honeycomb
your hair!**

Knock Knock!
Who's there?
Don.
Don who?
**Don just stand there!
Say something!**

Knock Knock!
Who's there?
Lulu.
Lulu who?
**Lulu's not working.
Can I use yours?**

Knock Knock!
Who's there?
Tiss.
Tiss who?
**Tiss who is good for
blowing your nose!**

224

Knock Knock!
Who's there?
Honeybee.
Honeybee who?
**Honeybee a dear
and get me a drink!**

Knock Knock!
Who's there?
Dougy.
Dougy who?
**Dougy hole in
your garden!**

Knock Knock!
Who's there?
Pierre.
Pierre who?
**Pierre through the
keyhole, you'll see!**

Knock Knock!
Who's there?
Wafer.
Wafer who?
**Wafer a long
time, but now
I'm back!**

Doctor: You'll only have to wear glasses at work.

Patient: That's impossible.

Doctor: Why?

Patient: I'm a boxer.

Doctor, doctor, my breath smells like a cat.

Here, have some mousewash.

Doctor, doctor, I swallowed a book.

Sit down and tell me the whole story.

Doctor: How is the reducing diet.

Patient: Not good — I'm a poor loser.

Patient: I injured myself when I fell out of a tree.

Doctor: What were you doing in a tree?

Patient: I was sweeping the leaves.

Doctor, doctor, I feel like a bucket.

You do look a little pail.

Knock Knock!
Who's there?
Annette.
Annette who?
Annette to play tennis would be handy!

Knock Knock!
Who's there?
Ivan
Ivan who?
Ivan to suck your blood!

Knock Knock!
Who's there?
Throat.
Throat who?
Throat to me!

Knock Knock!
Who's there?
Dan.
Dan who?
Dandruff!

228

Knock Knock!
Who's there?
Woody.
Woody who?
Woody you like to know!

Knock Knock!
Who's there?
Adolf.
Adolf who?
Adolph ball hit me in de mowf. Dat's why I dawk dis way!

Knock Knock!
Who's there?
Jess.
Jess who?
Jess me and my shadow!

Knock Knock!
Who's there?
Harmony.
Harmony who?
Harmony knock knock jokes do you expect me to know?

Knock Knock!
Who's there?
Amsterdam.
Amsterdam who?
**Amsterdam tired
of all these stupid
knock knock jokes!**

Knock Knock!
Who's there?
Tennessee.
Tennessee who?
**Tennessee you
tonight!**

Knock Knock!
Who's there?
Hugo.
Hugo who?
**Hugo jump in
the lake!**

Knock Knock!
Who's there?
Quiet Tina.
Quiet Tina who?
**Quiet Tina
classroom!**

230

Knock Knock!
Who's there?
Penguin.
Penguin who?
Penguin swimming!

Knock Knock!
Who's there?
Whoopi.
Whoopi who?
Whoopi cushion!

Knock Knock!
Who's there?
Tunis.
Tunis who?
Tunis company, three's a crowd!

Knock Knock!
Who's there?
Owl.
Owl who?
Owl be back later!

Doctor: Tell me, how long have you thought you're a ghost?

Patient: Ever since I started walking through walls.

Optician (holding a dinner plate): What is this?

Patient: I can't tell if it's a 5p or a 10p.

Doctor: I told you not to come out of doors.

Patient: I didn't — I came out the window.

Patient: How much is it to have a tooth taken out?

Dentist: Thirty pounds.

Patient: What, for three seconds' work?

Dentist: Ok, I'll tako it out slowly.

Doctor, doctor, I can only breathe in short pants.

Have you tried in long trousers?

Knock Knock!
Who's there?
Helium.
Helium who?
Helium, ah, um, ah, have to go!

Knock Knock!
Who's there?
Who.
Who who?
Who who hip who ray!

Knock Knock!
Who's there?
Cindy.
Cindy who?
Cindy fire engine fast!

Knock Knock!
Who's there?
Ada.
Ada who?
Ada enough now!

Knock Knock!
Who's there?
Acid.
Acid who?
Acid down and be quiet!

Knock Knock!
Who's there?
Tibet!
Tibet who?
Early Tibet and early to rise!

Knock Knock!
Who's there?
Tiffany!
Tiffany who?
Tiffany rubbish out the bin, will you?

Knock Knock!
Who's there?
Hammond.
Hammond who?
Hammond eggs!

Why did the fly fly?
Because the spider spied 'er!

Why did the firefly keep stealing things?

He was light fingered!

What goes 'snap, crackle and pop'?

A firefly with a short circuit!

Which fly makes films?

Steven Spielbug!

Why were the flies playing football in a saucer?

They were playing for the cup!

How do fireflies start a race?

Ready, steady, glow!

If there are five flies in the kitchen, how do you know which one is the American Football player?

It's the one in the sugar bowl!

What did one firefly say to the other?

'Got to glow now!'

Patient: Has the doctor sent the sleeping pill yet?

Nurse: Not yet, Sir.

Patient: Well, tell him to hurry up — I can hardly stay awake.

Doctor, doctor, I think I'm invisible.

Are you feeling faint?

Doctor, doctor, I keep hearing numbers instead of words.

It must be something you eight.

Patient: Can you tell me where the nearest hospital is?

Man: I don't know, but if you step in front of that car you'll get there.

Doctor: Vaccinations, then! Show me your right arm.

Patient: But I only washed the left one.

Doctor, doctor, I think I'm a fisherman.

Drop me a line, would you?

What is green, sooty and whistles when it rubs its back legs together?

Chimney Cricket!

What is a grasshopper?

An insect on a pogo stick!

Where do freshwater fish keep their savings?

In a river bank.

What's worse than a camel with backache?

A millipede with athlete's foot!

Which bird can lift the heaviest weight?

A crane.

What is the best year for kangaroos?

A leap year.

What do you call a bear without an ear?

B!

What is green and can jump a mile in a minute?

A grasshopper with hiccups!

Knock Knock!
Who's there?
Sarah.
Sarah who?
Sarah grown-up
in the house?

Knock Knock!
Who's there?
Dawn.
Dawn who?
Dawn do anything
I wouldn't do!

Knock Knock!
Who's there?
Wilfred.
Wilfred who?
Wilfred like his
present?

Knock Knock!
Who's there?
Chooch.
Chooch who?
There's a train
coming! All aboard!

242

Doctor, doctor, I keep hearing things when I first open my eyes.

What do you hear?

My alarm clock.

Doctor, doctor, I keep seeing into the future.

When did this happen?

Next Thursday.

Doctor, doctor, I feel spaced out.

What is your job?

I'm an astronaut.

What do you get if you cross a dog with a kangaroo?

A dog that has somewhere to put its own lead!

What do you get if you cross a dog and a sheep?

A sheep that can round itself up!

What do you get if you cross a dog and a lion?

A terrified postman!

What do you get if you cross two young dogs with a pair of headphones?

Hush puppies!

What do you get if you cross a dog with a frog?

A dog that can lick you from the other side of the road!

What do you call a litter of young dogs who have come in from the snow?

Slush puppies!

What do you call a dog with no legs?

It doesn't matter what you call him, he still won't come!

What makes a glow-worm glow?

A light meal!

What kind of doctors are like spiders?

Spin doctors!

What is the difference between a flea-bitten dog and a bored visitor?

One's going to itch and the other is itching to go!

Why are spiders like tops?

They are always spinning!

What has eight legs and likes living in trees?

Four orang-utans.

What did
the wife spider say
to her husband when
he tried to explain
why he was late?

'You're spinning me
a yarn here!'

What is the
difference between
school dinners and a
pile of slugs?

School dinners come
on a plate!

What did the slug
say as he slipped
down the wall?

'How slime flies!'

How do you know your
kitchen floor is dirty?

The slugs leave
a trail on the floor
that reads 'clean me'!

Optician: How many lines can you see on the chart?

Patient: Chart? What chart?

Doctor, doctor, I keep seeing spots before my eyes when I play games.

Which games are you playing?

Dominoes.

Doctor: Not many people live through this operation. Is there anything I can get you?

Patient: Yes, my coat.

Optician: Has your little boy got used to his glasses?

Mother: He won't wear them during the day, but I can slip them on him when he's asleep.

Doctor: Take one of these after each meal.

Patient: Do you prescribe the meals?

Doctor: Did you keep both windows open as I told you?

Patient: Well, there's only one window, so I opened it twice.

Why did the sparrow
go to the library?

It was looking for
bookworms!

What is life like
for a woodworm?

Boring!

How do you feel
if you cross a
sheepdog with
a melon?

Melon-collie!

Why can't you give
Elsa a balloon?

She will let it go!

What do you get if you cross a cocker spaniel, a poodle and a rooster?

Cockerpoodledoo!

What do you call a sheepdog's tail that can tell tall stories?

A shaggy dog's tale!

Why did the dog have a gleam in his eye?

Someone bumped his elbow while he was brushing his teeth.

Why do dogs run in circles?

Because it's hard to run in squares!

How did the little Scottish dog feel when he saw a monster?

Terrier-fied!

How do you find your dog if he's lost in the woods?

Put your ear up to a tree and listen for the bark!

Eleven dogs shared one umbrella, yet none got wet. How?

It wasn't raining.

How can you tell a dog from a jar of peanut butter?

The dog doesn't stick to the roof of your mouth.

260

How can you tell a
dog from a tomato?

The tomato
is red.

How can you
tell a dog from
an elephant?

The elephant
remembers.

What happened
when the lion ate
the comedian?

He felt funny.

How did the
dog make
anti-freeze?

He stole her blanket.

Patient: I'm travelling to India — are there any illnesses I should be aware of?

Doctor: Yes, india-gestion.

Doctor, doctor, I think I'm a sword swallower.

Here, take this iron tonic.

Doctor, doctor, I keep trying to get into fights.

And how long have you had this complaint?

Who wants to know?

Doctor, doctor, I can't pronounce my Fs, Ts, and Hs.

Well, you can't say fairer than that then, can you?

Doctor, doctor, during my operation I heard the surgeon use a four-letter word that upset me very much.

What word was that?

Oops.

Doctor, doctor, I've got a splitting headache.

Try this glue.

Knock Knock!
Who's there?
Wheelbarrow.
Wheelbarrow who?
Wheelbarrow some money and go on holiday!

Knock Knock!
Who's there?
Benny.
Benny who?
Bonny long time since I saw you!

Knock Knock!
Who's there?
Lena.
Lena who?
Lena a little closer and I'll tell you!

Knock Knock!
Who's there?
Zippy.
Zippy who?
Zippy dee-doo-dah, zippy dee hey!

Knock Knock!
Who's there?
Lee King.
Lee King who?
Lee King bucket!

Knock Knock!
Who's there?
Tennis.
Tennis who?
Tennis five plus five!

Knock Knock!
Who's there?
Eames.
Eames who?
Eames to please!

Knock Knock!
Who's there?
Utica.
Utica who?
**Utica the high road
and I'll take the
low road!**

Knock Knock!
Who's there?
Hand.
Hand who?
Hand over your wallet, this is a stick up!

Knock Knock!
Who's there?
Thayer.
Thayer who?
Thayer thorry and I won't throw this pie in your face!

Knock Knock!
Who's there?
Barry.
Barry who?
Barry the treasure where no one will find it!

266

Knock Knock!
Who's there?
Urchin.
Urchin who?
Urchin is pointy!

Knock Knock!
Who's there?
Beezer.
Beezer who?
Beezer black and yellow and make honey!

Knock Knock!
Who's there?
Weirdo.
Weirdo who?
Weirdo you think you're going?

Knock Knock!
Who's there?
UCI.
UCI who?
UCI had to ring because you didn't answer when I knocked!

Doctor: Can you tell me how you felt when you found out that you were ill?

Patient: Great — I didn't have to go to work.

Doctor, doctor, I feel like a clock.

Are you winding me up?

Doctor: Have you seen any little boys ring my bell and run away?

Policeman: No, they were grown men.

Doctor, doctor, I have a sore stomach. I ate three red snooker balls, two white snooker balls and four black snooker balls.

I see your problem — not enough greens.

Doctor: Why have you got a fried egg on your head?

Patient: Because the boiled one keeps falling off.

269

Knock Knock!
Who's there?
Falafel.
Falafel who?
Falafel off his bike and hurt his knee!

Knock Knock!
Who's there?
John.
John who?
John the Navy!

Knock Knock!
Who's there?
Daisy.
Daisy who?
Daisy that you are in, but I don't believe them!

Knock Knock!
Who's there?
UB40.
UB40 who?
UB40 today. Happy birthday!

Knock Knock!
Who's there?
Gerald.
Gerald who?
Gerald washed up!

Knock Knock!
Who's there?
Sam.
Sam who?
Sam person who knocked on the door last time!

Knock Knock!
Who's there?
Lucretia.
Lucretia who?
Lucretia from the Black Lagoon!

Knock Knock!
Who's there?
Titus.
Titus who?
Titus it can be!

Knock Knock!
Who's there?
Valencia.
Valencia who?
Valencia pound.
When will I get it
back?

Knock Knock!
Who's there?
Foster.
Foster who?
Foster than a
speeding bullet!

Knock Knock!
Who's there?
Les.
Les who?
Les go for a swim!

Knock Knock!
Who's there?
Garden.
Garden who?
Garden the treasure!

Knock Knock!
Who's there?
Sherlock.
Sherlock who?
Sherlock your door!
Someone could break in ...

Knock Knock!
Who's there?
Actor.
Actor who?
Actor you, my dear!

Doctor: You wrote to me to say you have flu, but now you say you have rheumatism.

Patient: I couldn't spell rheumatism.

Doctor, doctor, I feel like a car.

Stop driving me round the bend.

Doctor, doctor, my legs feel like jelly.

Don't worry, they'll be better in a trifle.

Doctor, doctor,
I feel like a thermostat.

Control yourself, will you?

Doctor, doctor, I
swallowed a clock
last week.

Why didn't you see
me before?

I didn't want to
alarm you.

Doctor: I don't like
that cold of yours.

Patient: Sorry, it's
the only one I've got.

Knock Knock!
Who's there?
Sadie.
Sadie who?
Sadie alphabet backwards!

Knock Knock!
Who's there?
Jacklyn.
Jacklyn who?
Jacklyn Hyde!

Knock Knock!
Who's there?
Major.
Major who?
Major headache, please gimme aspirin!

Knock Knock!
Who's there?
Gary.
Gary who?
Gary on smiling!

Knock Knock!
Who's there?
K-2.
K-2 who?
K-2 come in!

Knock Knock!
Who's there?
Hacienda.
Hacienda who?
Hacienda the story!

Knock Knock!
Who's there?
Knock knock!
Who's there?
Knock Knock!
Who's there?
I'm sorry, but my mother doesn't allow me to speak to strangers!

Knock Knock!
Who's there?
Manny.
Manny who?
Manny people keep asking me that!

Knock Knock!
Who's there?
Zombie.
Zombie who?
Zombies make honey, others are queens!

Knock Knock!
Who's there?
Knee.
Knee who?
Knee-d you ask?

Knock Knock!
Who's there?
Pasta.
Pasta who?
Pasta salt, please!

Knock Knock!
Who's there?
Raoul.
Raoul who?
Raoul with the punches!

Knock Knock!
Who's there?
Meg.
Meg who?
Meg me a drink!

Knock Knock!
Who's there?
Russian.
Russian who?
Russian about makes me tired!

Knock Knock!
Who's there?
Japan.
Japan who?
Japan is too hot, ouch!

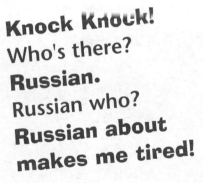

Doctor: Have you been taking that medicine?

Patient: No, I tasted it and decided I'd rather cough.

Doctor, doctor, I feel like a ladder.

Let's take this one step at a time.

Doctor, doctor, what will you give me for my sore throat?

Nothing, I don't want it.

Doctor: Please breathe out three times.

Patient: Is that to check my lungs?

Doctor: No, I need to clean my glasses.

Doctor, doctor, I feel like a clown.

Stop fooling yourself.

Doctor, doctor, I've eaten something that disagrees with me.

No you haven't.

Knock Knock!
Who's there?
Yacht.
Yacht who?
Yacht a know me by now!

Knock Knock!
Who's there?
Nine.
Nine who?
Nine danke!

Knock Knock!
Who's there?
Phoebe.
Phoebe who?
Phoebe too high for us to pay!

Knock Knock!
Who's there?
Miss Piggy.
Miss Piggy who?
Miss Piggy went to market, Miss Piggy stayed at home ...

Knock Knock!
Who's there?
Juno.
Juno who?
I dunno, Juno?

Knock Knock!
Who's there?
Moira.
Moira who?
The Moira the merrier!

Knock Knock!
Who's there?
Xena.
Xena who?
Xena minute!

Knock Knock!
Who's there?
Germaine.
Germaine who?
Germaine you don't recognise me?

Knock Knock!
Who's there?
Sharon!
Sharon who?
Sharon share alike!

Knock Knock!
Who's there?
Percy.
Percy who?
Percy-vere and you'll succeed!

Knock Knock!
Who's there?
Iraq.
Iraq who?
Iraq of lamb!

Knock Knock!
Who's there?
Dwayne.
Dwayne who?
Dwayne the bath tub, I'm drowning!

Knock Knock!
Who's there?
Mistake.
Mistake who?
**Mistake medicine
if you are poorly!**

Knock Knock!
Who's there?
Shower.
Shower who?
**Shower you care,
send her sumo
chocolates!**

Knock Knock!
Who's there?
Germany.
Germany who?
**Germany people
knocking on
your door?**

Knock Knock!
Who's there?
Oui.
Oui who?
**Oui will, oui
will, rock you!**

Doctor, doctor, I think I'm a bee.

Take this and if it doesn't work give me a buzz.

Doctor, doctor, I feel like a snooker ball.

Get to the end of the cue.

Doctor, doctor, I've gone a funny colour.

Don't worry — it's just a pigment of your imagination.

Patient: I swallowed a bone.

Doctor: Are you choking?

Patient: No, I really did!

Doctor, doctor, I feel
like a banana.

Come back tomorrow
and I'll try to slip you in.

How did the dog
make gold soup?

He put in 24 carrots.

How did the dog's
owner know his pet
was angry about
having soap flakes
for breakfast?

He foamed at
the mouth.

How do you
keep a dog from
barking in your
front garden?

Put him in your
back garden.

How do you make a
dog float?

Take two scoops of
ice cream, some
fizzy drink and a
small dog.

How is a
cowardly dog
like a
leaky tap?

They both run.

How is a dog like a penny?

They both have a
head and a tail.

What do you
call a very
rude bird?

A mockingbird.

Which birds steal
soap from baths?

Robber ducks!

Why did the moth nibble a hole in the carpet?

He wanted to see the floor show!

What's the biggest moth in the world?

A mammoth!

Why was the moth so unpopular?

He kept picking holes in everything!

What did the spider say when he broke his new web?

Darn it!

What is a myth?
A female moth!

What happened
when the chef found
a daddy long legs in
the salad?

It became a daddy
short legs!

What do you
get if you cross
a tarantula with
a rose?

I'm not sure, but
I wouldn't try
smelling it.

Why did the spider
buy a car?

So he could take it
out for a spin!

Patient: My wife mistook that medicine for furniture polish.

Doctor: Do you need some more?

Patient: No, I want you to shake our table.

Doctor, doctor, what's the axe on the wall for?

It's for splitting headaches.

Doctor, doctor, I feel like a pop star.

Nurse, get his records.

Doctor, doctor, my head feels like a lump of lead, my neck is as stiff as a poker and I feel like I have bands of iron around my chest.

You don't need a doctor, you need a blacksmith.

Doctor, doctor, I have a terrible corn on the bottom of my foot.

That's a good place to have it — no one else can step on it.

Knock Knock!
Who's there?
Iris.
Iris who?
Iris Tew in the name of the law!

Knock Knock!
Who's there?
Unite.
Unite who?
Unite a person, then call him Sir!

Knock Knock!
Who's there?
Goblin.
Goblin who?
Goblin your candy will make your tummy ache!

Knock Knock!
Who's there?
Hannah.
Hannah who?
Hannah Happy New Year!

Knock Knock!
Who's there?
Barbara.
Barbara who?
Barbara, black sheep, have you any wool?

Knock Knock!
Who's there?
Cereal.
Cereal who?
Cereal pleasure to meet you!

Knock Knock!
Who's there?
Hiram.
Hiram who?
Hiram fine, how are you?

Knock Knock!
Who's there?
Felix.
Felix who?
Felix-cited all over!

Where would you put an injured insect?

In an antbulance!

What do you get if you cross the Lone Ranger with an insect?

The masked-quito!

What has antlers and sucks blood?

A moose-quito!

Why did the mosquito go to the dentist?

To improve his bite!

What is a mosquito's
favourite sport?

Skin-diving!

How do you know
if you have a tough
mosquito?

You slap him and he
slaps you back!

What is the
difference between
a mosquito
and a fly?

Try sewing buttons
on a mosquito!

What's the difference
between a zombie
and a mosquito?

A mosquito drops off
you when you die!

Doctor, doctor, I haven't slept for days.

What's the matter?

Nothing, I sleep at night.

Doctor, doctor, my boss sacked me for medical reasons.

What's wrong with you?

Nothing — he was sick of me.

Doctor, doctor, I swallowed a plank of wood.

How do you feel?

Board stiff.

Doctor, doctor, I keep
dreaming I'm being
followed by a snowman.

Stand by the radiator and
your dreams will melt away.

Doctor, doctor, I feel
like an ice cream.

Here's £1 — get me
one too.

Doctor, doctor, I'm having
a problem with those
strengthening tablets.

What's wrong?

I can't get the lid
off the jar.

Knock Knock!
Who's there?
Ask me.
Ask me who?
Ask me inside and you'll find out!

Knock Knock!
Who's there?
Mustard.
Mustard who?
Mustard left it in the car!

Knock Knock!
Who's there?
Ireland.
Ireland who?
Ireland you some money if you promise to pay me back!

Knock Knock!
Who's there?
Rapunzel.
Rapunzel who?
Rapunzel troubles in your old kitbag and smile, smile, smile!

300

Knock Knock!
Who's there?
Poker.
Poker who?
**Poker and see
if she's awake!**

Knock Knock!
Who's there?
Isaac.
Isaac who?
**Isaac'ly who do
you think this is?**

Knock Knock!
Who's there?
Ivory.
Ivory who?
**Ivory strong
like Tarzan!**

Knock Knock!
Who's there?
Owl.
Owl who?
**Owl I can say is
'Knock, knock!'**

What's a glow-worm's favourite song?

Wake me up before you glow-glow!

Why was the glow-worm unhappy?

Because her children weren't that bright!

What do you get if you cross a glow-worm with some beer?

Light ale!

What do you get if you cross a worm and a young goat?

A dirty kid!

What do worms leave around their baths?

The scum of the earth!

What did one maggot say to another?

'What's a nice maggot like you doing in a joint like this!'

What did the woodworm say to the chair?

'It's been nice gnawing you!'

What's yellow, wriggles and is dangerous?

A maggot with attitude!

Doctor: Have you been waiting long?

Patient: Well, did you know there are 217,989 spots on the waiting room wallpaper?

Doctor, doctor, there's a mist in front of my eyes – what can it be?

I haven't the foggiest idea.

Doctor, doctor, I swallowed some sandpaper.

How do you feel?

Pretty rough.

Doctor: Have you been counting sheep to fall asleep?

Patient: Well, I counted to 18,000.

Doctor: Did it work?

Patient: No, it was time to get up.

Doctor, doctor, I can't swim. What should I do?

I can't play the piano, but I'm not complaining.

Knock Knock!
Who's there?
Urinal.
Urinal who?
Urinal lot of trouble!

Knock Knock!
Who's there?
Pepperoni.
Pepperoni who?
Pepperoni makes me sneeze!

Knock Knock!
Who's there?
Izzy.
Izzy who?
Izzy come, Izzy go!

Knock Knock!
Who's there?
Me.
Me who?
Meeow!

Knock Knock!
Who's there?
Salmon.
Salmon who?
Salmon enchanted evening!

Knock Knock!
Who's there?
Pickle.
Pickle who?
Pickle little flower and give it to your mother!

Knock Knock!
Who's there?
Hodedofo.
Hodedofo who?
Hodedofo me, my arms are full!

How do you catch a runaway dog?

Hide behind a tree and make a noise like a bone!

What dog loves to take bubble baths?

A shampoodle!

What kind of dog does a vampire prefer?

Any kind of bloodhound!

What dogs are best for sending telegrams?

Wire-haired terriers.

What is a dog's favourite city?

New Yorkie!

Who is a dog's favourite comedian?

Growlcho Marx!

What did the cowboy say when the bear ate Lassie?

'Well, doggone!'

What do you get if you take a really big dog out for a walk?

A great dane out!

Doctor, doctor, I'm putting on weight.

Take regular exercise.

What sort of exercise?

Push yourself away from the dinner table.

Doctor: I'm going to take your pulse.

Patient: Why — haven't you got one of your own?

Doctor, doctor, I feel like a biscuit.

Sit down — I won't eat you.

Athlete: What's my temperature?

Doctor: One hundred and one.

Athlete: What's the world record?

Doctor, doctor, my knees won't stop shaking. What can I do?

Tie a pair of cymbals to your legs and start a one-man band.

Doctor, doctor, I feel like a dishcloth.

Take these tablets and I'll give you a wring in the morning.

Knock Knock!
Who's there?
Paul.
Paul who?
Paul a fast one!

Knock Knock!
Who's there?
Armageddon.
Armageddon who?
Armageddon out of here!

Knock Knock!
Who's there?
Courtney.
Courtney who?
Courtney burglars recently!

Knock Knock!
Who's there?
Genoa.
Genoa who?
Genoa any new knock knock jokes?

Knock Knock!
Who's there?
Steve.
Steve who?
Steve upper lip!

Knock Knock!
Who's there?
Douglas.
Douglas who?
Douglas is broken!

Knock Knock!
Who's there?
Luke.
Luke who?
Luke before you leap!

Knock Knock!
Who's there?
Noah.
Noah who?
Noah-body knows the trouble I go through!

Knock Knock!
Who's there?
Paula.
Paula who?
Paula up the door handle, will you, and let me in!

Knock Knock!
Who's there?
Gerald.
Gerald who?
Gerald friend (Insert name)!

Knock Knock!
Who's there?
Bingo.
Bingo who?
Bingo'ing to come and see you for ages!

Knock Knock!
Who's there?
Jenny.
Jenny who?
Jenny'd some help opening the door, it's taking you long enough!

Knock Knock!
Who's there?
Horace.
Horace who?
Horace-scopes can be fun!

Knock Knock!
Who's there?
Dozen.
Dozen who?
Dozen anybody want to play with me?

Knock Knock!
Who's there?
Heart.
Heart who?
Heart to hear you, speak up a bit!

Knock Knock!
Who's there?
Amnesia.
Amnesia who?
Oh, I see you have it too!

Doctor, doctor, I think I'm a piece of string — I've felt like this for months.

Why didn't you come and see me before?

I was a bit tied up.

What time do you go to the dentist?

Tooth-hurty.

Doctor: Where's the next patient?

Nurse: She didn't look very well so I sent her home.

Patient: How much to have three teeth out?

Dentist: Ninety pounds.

Patient: Forget it — I'll pick a fight on the way home.

Doctor (to butcher): The meat you sold me tastes awful.

Butcher: So did the medicine you gave me.

Doctor, doctor, I feel like a tub of margarine.

Well, spread yourself out on the couch.

Knock Knock!
Who's there?
Armada.
Armada who?
Armada told us there'd be days like this.

Knock Knock!
Who's there?
Mary Queen of Scots.
Mary Queen of Scots who?
Mary Queen of Scots who? Didn't you learn anything in history class?

Knock Knock!
Who's there?
Whij.
Whij who?
Whij one of you locked the door?

Knock Knock!
Who's there?
Turnip.
Turnip who?
Turnip the radio, please!

Knock Knock!
Who's there?
Teresa.
Teresa who?
Teresa green!

Knock Knock!
Who's there?
Abbey.
Abbey who?
Abbey birthday to you!

Knock Knock!
Who's there?
Halibut.
Halibut who?
Halibut a kiss, sweetie?

Knock Knock!
Who's there?
Earl.
Earl who?
Earl be glad to get to bed, I'm tired!

Knock Knock!
Who's there?
Yukon.
Yukon who?
Yukon say that again!

Knock Knock!
Who's there?
Bab.
Bab who?
Bab-boon is a real ape!

Knock Knock!
Who's there?
Earwig.
Earwig who?
Earwigo, earwigo, earwigo!

Knock Knock!
Who's there?
Texas.
Texas who?
Texas are getting higher every year!

Knock Knock!
Who's there?
Bed.
Bed who?
Bed you can't guess I've got a cold!

Knock Knock!
Who's there?
Toronto.
Toronto who?
Toronto be a law against these knock knock jokes!

Knock Knock!
Who's there?
Walnuts.
Walnuts who?
Walnuts around here!

Doctor, doctor, skin trouble has given me a broken arm.

How's that?

It was a banana skin.

Doctor, doctor, I think I'm a newspaper.

Take these pills — they'll improve your circulation.

Doctor, doctor, you've broken your arm in three places.

How? I've only been in one place.

Doctor, doctor, I have trouble getting up in the morning.

I'm prescribing you yeast and shoe polish — it'll help you rise and shine.

Doctor, doctor, my brother thinks he's an orange.

Tell him to come and see me.

It's OK, he's here in my pocket.

Doctor: You need more exercise — you should try walking.

Patient: But, doctor, I'm a postman.

Knock Knock!
Who's there?
Hammond.
Hammond who?
Hammond cheese on toast, please!

Knock Knock!
Who's there?
Crispin.
Crispin who?
Crispin crunchy is how I like my apples!

Knock Knock!
Who's there?
Odysseus.
Odysseus who?
Odysseus the last straw!

Knock Knock!
Who's there?
Ridya.
Ridya who?
Ridya bike and you'll get there quicker!

Knock Knock!
Who's there?
Wizard.
Wizard who?
Wizard you I'm lost!

Knock Knock!
Who's there?
Earlier.
Earlier who?
Earlier fly is undone!

Knock Knock!
Who's there?
Anderson.
Anderson who?
**Anderson and
daughter came too!**

325

Knock Knock!
Who's there?
Bean.
Bean who?
Bean working very hard today!

Knock Knock!
Who's there?
Watusi.
Watusi who?
Watusi is what you get!

Knock Knock!
Who's there?
Edith.
Edith who?
Edith, it'll make you feel better!

Knock Knock!
Who's there?
Thumb.
Thumb who?
Thumb like it hot, thumb like it cold!

Knock Knock!
Who's there?
Carol.
Carol who?
Carol go if you turn the ignition key!

Knock Knock!
Who's there?
Tyrone.
Tyrone who?
Tyrone shoelaces!

Knock Knock!
Who's there?
Danielle.
Danielle who?
Danielle at me, it's not my fault!

Optician: How did your eyesight get so bad?

Patient: I was reading a book about how to avoid eye strain.

What do you get when you add thirteen patients to thirteen patients?

Twenty sicks.

Doctor: Sorry, my hours are between two and five.

Patient: Tell that to the dog that bit me.

Doctor: Did you drink that water an hour before breakfast, as I told you?

Patient: I tried, but I couldn't keep it up for more than five minutes.

Doctor, doctor, I feel like a crystal ball.

Sit down and I'll look into this.

Doctor, doctor, I feel like a tree.

Don't worry, we'll get to the root of the problem.

Knock Knock!
Who's there?
Hans.
Hans who?
Hans off the table!

Knock Knock!
Who's there?
Michelle.
Michelle who?
Michelle sea shells on the sea shore!

Knock Knock!
Who's there?
Billy.
Billy who?
Billy goat gruff!

Knock Knock!
Who's there?
Marmite.
Marmite who?
Marmite but Pa won't!

Knock Knock!
Who's there?
Bertha.
Bertha who?
**Bertha day
greetings!**

Knock Knock!
Who's there?
Tuba.
Tuba who?
Tuba toothpaste!

Knock Knock!
Who's there?
Harlow.
Harlow who?
Harlow will you go!

Knock Knock!
Who's there?
Hugo.
Hugo who?
Hugo to bed now!

Knock Knock!
Who's there?
Dana.
Dana who?
Dana talk with your mouth full!

Knock Knock!
Who's there?
Patty O.
Patty O who?
Patty O furniture!

Knock Knock!
Who's there?
Sweden.
Sweden who?
Sweden sour is my favourite Chinese meal!

Knock Knock!
Who's there?
Boxer.
Boxer who?
Boxer tricks!

Knock Knock!
Who's there?
Goose.
Goose who?
Goose who's knocking!

Knock Knock!
Who's there?
Sari.
Sari who?
Sari I was sarong!

Knock Knock!
Who's there?
Dai.
Dai who?
Dai Larfin.

Knock Knock!
Who's there?
Stew.
Stew who?
Stew early to go to bed!

Doctor: You should take a bath before you retire.

Patient: But I don't retire for another thirty years.

Doctor, doctor, I can't stop laughing.

Ah, that'll be your funny bone.

Doctor, doctor, can you help me? My name is Bertha Bigbottom.

Sorry, I can't do anything about that.

Doctor: You're looking a lot better.

Patient: Yes, I followed the instructions on the bottle you gave me.

Doctor: What did they say?

Patient: Keep tightly corked.

Doctor, doctor, I feel like the moon.

I can't see you now, come back tonight.

Knock Knock!
Who's there?
Emma.
Emma who?
Emma glad you asked me that!

Knock Knock!
Who's there?
Carrie.
Carrie who?
Carrie me home, I'm tired!

Knock Knock!
Who's there?
Harold.
Harold who?
Harold are you?

Knock Knock!
Who's there?
Abel.
Abel who.
Abel seaman!

Knock Knock!
Who's there?
Wanda.
Wanda who?
**Wanda have
another drink?**

Knock Knock!
Who's there?
Ellis.
Ellis who?
Ellis before 'M'!

Knock Knock!
Who's there?
Kaye.
Kaye who?
Kaye sera sera!

Knock Knock!
Who's there?
Puss.
Puss who?
Puss your bike, it's safer!

Knock Knock!
Who's there?
Hijack.
Hijack who?
Hijack, how's Jill?

Knock Knock!
Who's there?
Elsie.
Elsie who?
Elsie you around!

Knock Knock!
Who's there?
Laurie.
Laurie who?
Laurie driver!

Knock Knock!
Who's there?
Fozzie.
Fozzie who?
Fozzie hundreth time, my name is Ben!

Knock Knock!
Who's there?
Mica.
Mica who?
Mica is double parked!

Knock Knock!
Who's there?
Philippa.
Philippa who?
**Philippa bath tub,
I'm dirty!**

Knock Knock!
Who's there?
Heidi.
Heidi who?
**Heidi-clare war
on you!**

Knock Knock!
Who's there?
Ewan.
Ewan who?
No, just me!

Doctor: I'm afraid you have pneumonia pneumonia.

Patient: What's that?

Doctor: It's double pneumonia.

Doctor, doctor, I have an infectious laugh.

Don't laugh near me then.

Optician: Can you read the word on the chart?

Patient: Oh yes — I just can't pronounce it.

Dentist: I'll have to charge you fifty pounds for extracting that tooth.

Patient: But I thought you charged ten pounds.

Dentist: I do, but your screams frightened off my other patients.

Which part of the body tells lies?

The fibula.

Knock Knock!
Who's there?
Butcher.
Butcher who?
Butcher left leg in,
your left leg out!

Knock Knock!
Who's there?
Alan.
Alan who?
Alan't my lesson!

Knock Knock!
Who's there?
Hey.
Hey who?
Hey ho, hey ho, it's
off to work we go!

342

Knock Knock!
Who's there?
Lady.
Lady who?
Lady law down!

Knock Knock!
Who's there?
Kipper.
Kipper who?
**Kipper hands
to yourself!**

Knock Knock!
Who's there?
Bug.
Bug who?
Bug-sy Malone!

Knock Knock!
Who's there?
Boo.
Boo who?
**Just boo.
I'm a ghost!**

Knock Knock!
Who's there?
Fitzwilliam.
Fitzwilliam who?
Fitzwilliam better than it fits me!

Knock Knock!
Who's there?
Custer.
Custer who?
Custer penny to find out!

Knock Knock!
Who's there?
Michelle.
Michelle who?
Micholle had a big crab inside it!

Knock Knock!
Who's there?
Lucinda.
Lucinda who?
Lucinda chain, I want to get in!

Knock Knock!
Who's there?
Tobias.
Tobias who?
Tobias a pig, that's why I went to market!

Knock Knock!
Who's there?
Janet.
Janet who?
Janet has too many holes in it, the fish will escape!

Knock Knock!
Who's there?
Paul.
Paul who?
Paul hard, the door's stuck again!

Knock Knock!
Who's there?
Midas.
Midas who?
Midas well open the door!

Doctor: What's the matter with you?

Cannibal patient: Indigestion — I just ate a millionaire.

Doctor: I told you to avoid rich food.

Nurse: I bet your wife misses you a lot.

Patient: No, her aim's very good — that's why I'm here.

Doctor, doctor, I've got a splinter in my finger.

Been scratching your head again, have you?

Doctor: Have you been anywhere else?

Patient: I went to the chemist.

Doctor: And what stupid advice did he give you?

Patient: He told me to come and see you.

Doctor: Did you take my advice and sleep with the windows open.

Patient: Yes, and I got burgled.

Knock Knock!
Who's there?
Bruce.
Bruce who?
I bruce easily, be gentle!

Knock Knock!
Who's there?
Honeydew.
Honeydew who?
Honeydew you want to come out tonight?

Knock Knock!
Who's there?
Arthur.
Arthur who?
Arthur-mometer is good for measuring temperature!

Knock Knock!
Who's there?
Deena.
Deena who?
Deena you hear the first time?

Knock Knock!
Who's there?
Harold.
Harold who?
Harold do you think I look?

Knock Knock!
Who's there?
Sonia.
Sonia who?
Sonia paper boy making a delivery!

Knock Knock!
Who's there?
Colin.
Colin who?
Colin and see me on the way home!

Knock Knock!
Who's there?
Matt.
Matt who?
Mattadore!

Knock Knock!
Who's there?
Rocky.
Rocky who?
Rocky bye baby on the tree top!

Knock Knock!
Who's there?
Olaf.
Olaf who?
Olaf if you think it's funny!

Knock Knock!
Who's there?
Enoch.
Enoch who?
Enoch and enoch, but nobody opens the door!

Knock Knock!
Who's there?
Dinamite.
Dinamite who?
Dinamite if you ask her nicely!

Knock Knock!
Who's there?
Amy.
Amy who?
**Amy'fraid
I've forgotten!**

Knock Knock!
Who's there?
Roxanne.
Roxanne who?
**Roxanne pebbles are
all over the beach!**

Knock Knock!
Who's there?
Iris.
Iris who?
Iris you were here!

Knock Knock!
Who's there?
Tilly.
Tilly who?
Tilly what – open the door!

Doctor: How are your broken ribs?

Patient: OK, but I have a stitch in my side.

Doctor: Good — that means the bones are knitting.

Doctor, doctor, I feel like a brain.

I'm sure it's just in your head.

Doctor, doctor, I wounded myself on the way here.

I told you not to take the short cut.

Doctor: I think you should give up golf.

Patient: Is it bad for my health?

Doctor: No, you're just not very good.

Doctor, doctor, I've just swallowed a pen.

Well sit down and write your name.

Doctor, doctor, my nose is running.

Well, run after it.

Knock Knock!
Who's there?
York.
York who?
**York coming over
to our place!**

Knock Knock!
Who's there?
Meg.
Meg who?
**Meg your bed
before breakfast!**

Knock Knock!
Who's there?
**Heywood, Hugh and
Harry.**
Heywood Hugh and
Harry who?
**Heywood Hugh Harry
up and open the door!**

Knock Knock!
Who's there?
Lena.
Lena who?
**Lena little closer
and I'll tell you!**

Knock Knock!
Who's there?
Rhoda.
Rhoda who?
I rhoda camel to school and my teacher got the hump!

Knock Knock!
Who's there?
Mister.
Mister who?
I mister last bus home!

Knock Knock!
Who's there?
Diana.
Diana who?
Diana thirst, can I have some water please?

Knock Knock!
Who's there?
Eugenie.
Eugenie who?
Eugenie from the bottle, I'll give you three wishes!

Knock Knock!
Who's there?
Alice.
Alice who?
**Alice N. Tew if
you listen to me!**

Knock Knock!
Who's there?
Daryl.
Daryl who?
**Daryl never be
another you!**

Knock Knock!
Who's there?
Matthew.
Matthew who?
**Matthew lace has
come undone!**

Knock Knock!
Who's there?
Max.
Max who?
**Max no difference
to you, just let
me in!**

Knock Knock!
Who's there?
Bridget.
Bridget who?
London Bridget falling down, falling down.

Knock Knock!
Who's there?
Oscar.
Oscar who?
Oscar if she wants a drink!

Knock Knock!
Who's there?
Althea.
Althea who?
Althea later in the afternoon!

Knock Knock!
Who's there?
Toodle.
Toodle who?
Bye bye!

357

Doctor: Did the medicine I gave your brother straighten him out?

Patient: Oh yes, they buried him yesterday.

Doctor, doctor, I think I'm a pony.

No, you're just a little hoarse.

Why was the dentist always miserable?

Because he looks down in the mouth.

Doctor, doctor,
I went to the cowboy
festival and now I can't
stop coughing.

Mmm — you must
have bronco-itis.

Doctor, doctor, I
don't feel so hot.

That's because you
have a cold.

Why did the
doctor retire?

He ran out
of patience.

Knock Knock!
Who's there?
Europe.
Europe who?
**Europe early
this morning!**

Knock Knock!
Who's there?
Norman.
Norman who?
**Norman has ever set
foot in here before!**

Knock Knock!
Who's there?
Farmer.
Farmer who?
**Farmer people here
than there were
last year!**

Knock Knock!
Who's there?
Musket.
Musket who?
**Musket in, it's
urgent!**

Knock Knock!
Who's there?
Tuna.
Tuna who?
Tuna music down, I'm trying to sleep!

Knook Knock!
Who's there?
Hobbit.
Hobbit who?
Hobbit letting me in then!

Knock Knock!
Who's there?
Amanda.
Amanda who?
Amanda-rin!

Knock Knock!
Who's there?
Fido.
Fido who?
Fido I have to wait here!

Knock Knock!
Who's there?
Eliza.
Eliza who?
Eliza wake at night thinking about this door!

Knock Knock!
Who's there?
One-eye.
One-eye who?
You're the one-eye care for!

Knock Knock!
Who's there?
Pill.
Pill who?
Yes please, and a sheet to go with it!

Knock Knock!
Who's there?
Pencil.
Pencil who?
Your pencil fall down if the elastic goes!

362

Knock Knock!
Who's there?
Gutter.
Gutter who?
**Gutter get in, it's
freezing out here!**

Knock Knock!
Who's there?
Owen.
Owen who?
**Owen are you going
to let me in?**

Knock Knock!
Who's there?
Howell.
Howell who?
**Howell you have your toast,
marmalade or jam?**

Knock Knock!
Who's there?
Hayden.
Hayden who?
Hayden seek is fun to play!

If taking out your appendix is called an appendectomy and removing your tonsils is called a tonsillectomy, what is removing a growth from your head?

A haircut.

Doctor, doctor, my pet chicken is ill.

It's probably got people pox.

Doctor, doctor, I feel like a crocodile.

See you in a while ...

Doctor, doctor,
my pet crocodile
is sick.

Are you sure it's
not an illigator?

What did the doctor
say to the tonsil?

'You look nice, can I
take you out?'

Doctor, doctor, I
caught a cold coming
up in the lift.

No, no — you can
only come down
with a cold.

Knock Knock!
Who's there?
Ollie.
Ollie who?
Ollie time you do that I want to scream!

Knock Knock!
Who's there?
Denver.
Denver who?
Denver the good old days!

Knock Knock!
Who's there?
Hurd.
Hurd who?
Hurd my hand so I can't knock!

Knock Knock!
Who's there?
Odessa.
Odessa who?
Odessa really fun joke!

366

Knock Knock!
Who's there?
Tuna.
Tuna who?
Tuna violin and it will sound better!

Knock Knock!
Who's there?
Cynthia.
Cynthia who?
Cynthia been gone I miss you very much!

Knock Knock!
Who's there?
Murray.
Murray who?
Murray me! Not likely ...

Knock Knock!
Who's there?
Gus.
Gus who?
That's what you're supposed to do!

Why shouldn't you take an elephant to the zoo?

Because he'd rather go to the movies!

Where do little fish go every morning?

To plaice school!

Where do fish wash?

In a river basin!

What do you say to a mouse that's chipped its front tooth?

'Hard cheese.'

Why did the zebra cross the road?

To make a zebra crossing.

What is green, tasty and pecks on trees?

Woody Wood Pickle.

What do you call a bunch of chickens playing hide-and-seek?

Fowl play.

What's got six legs and can fly long distance?

Three swallows.

Doctor, doctor, I've got cold feet, a hot head and I can see spots in front of my eyes.

You're wearing your spotty socks on your head again.

Doctor, doctor, I keep thinking I'm a caterpillar.

Don't worry you'll soon change!

Doctor, doctor, my dog's swallowed a watch.

Another case of ticks, I suppose.

Doctor, doctor, did I tell you the one about the germs?

No, but don't spread it about.

Doctor, doctor, I've swallowed some uranium.

Have you got atomic ache?

Doctor, doctor, I've been hit by a snowball.

Were you knocked out cold?

Why is an optician like a teacher?

They both test the pupils.

Knock Knock!
Who's there?
Scissor.
Scissor who?
Scissor or Cleopatra!

Knock Knock!
Who's there?
Roland.
Roland who?
Roland stone gathers no moss!

Knock Knock!
Who's there?
Cannelloni.
Cannelloni who?
Cannelloni some money until next week?

Knock Knock!
Who's there?
Plato.
Plato who?
Plato fish and chips please!

Knock Knock!
Who's there?
Sofa.
Sofa who?
Sofa so good!

Knock Knock!
Who's there?
Cindy.
Cindy who?
Cindy next one in please!

Knock Knock!
Who's there?
Indonesia.
Indonesia who?
I get weak Indonesia when I look at you!

Knock Knock!
Who's there?
Dwight.
Dwight who?
Dwight stuff on your mouth!

Knock Knock!
Who's there?
Weevil.
Weevil who?
**Weevil only be
staying a minute!**

Knock Knock!
Who's there?
Pasture.
Pasture who?
**Pasture bed
time, isn't it?**

Knock Knock!
Who's there?
Otis.
Otis who?
**Otis a wonderful day
to walk in the park!**

Knock Knock!
Who's there?
Ella.
Ella who?
**Ella-vator. Doesn't
that give you a lift!**

374

Knock Knock!
Who's there?
Marmalade.
Marmalade who?
Marmalade me an egg for breakfast!

Knock Knock!
Who's there?
Dotty.
Dotty who?
Dotty way the cookie crumbles!

Knock Knock!
Who's there?
Spook.
Spook who?
Spook-etti!

Knock Knock!
Who's there?
Yulla.
Yulla who?
Yulla catch more flies with honey and vinegar!

Patient: Is the operation over?

Doctor: Yes — that's enough out of you.

Doctor, doctor, I've got acid indigestion.

Stop drinking acid.

Doctor, doctor, I feel like a ghost.

You seem in good spirits to me.

Doctor, doctor, I feel like a ship.

Come into the sick bay.

Doctor, doctor,
I can't stop
swearing.

Glad to hear you're
in rude health.

Doctor, doctor,
I feel like a ship.

I'm a doc, not
a dock.

Doctor, doctor,
I feel like a
racehorse.

Here, try these
Epsom salts.

Doctor, doctor, I
feel like a torch.

Could you enlighten
me further?

Knock Knock!
Who's there?
Holmes.
Holmes who?
Holmes where the heart is!

Knock Knock!
Who's there?
Ellie.
Ellie who?
Ellie-phants never forget!

Knock Knock!
Who's there?
Atlas.
Atlas who?
Atlas it's Friday, the weekend's nearly here!

Knock Knock!
Who's there?
Summertime.
Summertime who?
Summertime you're a pest!

378

Knock Knock!
Who's there?
Juicy.
Juicy who?
Juicy the sign on the door?

Knock Knock!
Who's there?
Atomic.
Atomic who?
Atomic ache!

Knock Knock!
Who's there?
Catskill.
Catskill who?
Catskill mice!

Knock Knock!
Who's there?
Illegals.
Illegals who?
Illegals stay in the nest until they feel better!

Knock Knock!
Who's there?
Seymour.
Seymour who?
Seymour if you look out the window!

Knock Knock!
Who's there?
Darius.
Darius who?
Darius a lot of things I have to tell you!

Knock Knock!
Who's there?
Francis.
Francis who?
Francis where people speak French!

Knock Knock!
Who's there?
Saul.
Saul who?
Saul the king's horses and saul the king's men!

Knock Knock!
Who's there?
Omega.
Omega who?
Omega the best man win!

Knock Knock!
Who's there?
Carlotta.
Carlotta who?
**Carlotta trouble
when it breaks
down!**

Knock Knock!
Who's there?
Emile.
Emile who?
Emile fit for a king!

Doctor, doctor, I feel like an abacus.

It'll soon pass, but I wouldn't count on it.

Doctor, doctor, I feel like an adjective.

Can you describe it for me?

What injections do astronauts have?

Rocket boosters.

Doctor, doctor, I feel like an artist.

OK, let's look at the bigger picture.

Doctor, doctor,
I feel like a
national anthem.

Look, I won't
stand for it.

Doctor, doctor, I feel
like a long story.

Ok, let's start at the
beginning.

Doctor, doctor,
I feel like an
anecdote.

When I was a boy ...

Knock Knock!
Who's there?
Alfalfa.
Alfalfa who?
Alfalfa you if you fall for me!

Knock Knock!
Who's there?
Yukon.
Yukon who?
Yukon fool some people all the time!

Knock Knock!
Who's there?
Walrus.
Walrus who?
Why do you walrus ask the same question?

Knock Knock!
Who's there?
Gopher.
Gopher who?
Gopher it and you might win!

Knock Knock!
Who's there?
Romeo.
Romeo who?
Romeo-ver to the other side of the lake!

Knock Knock!
Who's there?
Oslo.
Oslo who!
Oslo down, what's the hurry?

Knock Knock!
Who's there?
Fodder.
Fodder who?
Fodder and mother are taking me for a picnic!

Knock Knock!
Who's there?
Typhoid.
Typhoid who?
Typhoid that song before!

Knock Knock!
Who's there?
Cattle.
Cattle who?
Cattle always purr when you stroke it!

Knock Knock!
Who's there?
Spook.
Spook who?
Spook only when you are spoken to!

Knock Knock!
Who's there?
Aida.
Aida who?
Aida lot of green apples, now I feel sick!

Knock Knock!
Who's there?
Celeste.
Celeste who?
Celeste time I'm telling you! Open up!

Knock Knock!
Who's there?
Anatole.
Anatole who?
**Anatole me you're
so annoying!**

Knock Knock!
Who's there?
Frank Lee.
Frank Lee who?
**Frank Lee I
don't care!**

Knock Knock!
Who's there?
Acid.
Acid who?
**Acid-down and
be quiet!**

Knock Knock!
Who's there?
Chin up.
Chin up who?
**Chin up, I'm not
going to tell
any more knock
knock jokes!**

Doctor, doctor, I keep turning small piles of earth into huge lumps of rock.

I think you're making mountains out of molehills.

Doctor, doctor, I think I'm a bear.

Nurse! Call the zoo!

Doctor, doctor, I keep disagreeing with everyone.

Yes, you told me before.

No I didn't.

Doctor, doctor,
I feel like a
storyteller.

You're making
it all up.

Doctor, doctor, I
feel like a skeleton.

Could you flesh it
out for me?

Doctor, doctor,
I feel like Father
Christmas.

Could I have a new
bike please?

Why did the owl, 'owl?

Because the woodpecker would peck 'er!

What do parrots eat?

Pollyfilla.

Which animal is a really good driver?

A steer!

What do you call a crate of ducks?

A box of quackers.

What do you get if you cross a duck with a firework?

A firequacker.

What is the difference between a maggot and a cockroach?

Cockroaches crunch more when you eat them.

Why was the insect kicked out of the park?

Because he was a litterbug!

What do you give a sick bird?

Tweetment!

Knock Knock!
Who's there?
Bet.
Bet who?
Bet you don't know who's knocking!

Knock Knock!
Who's there?
Cologne.
Cologne who?
Cologne Ranger!

Knock Knock!
Who's there?
Gino.
Gino who?
Gino me? Open the door!

Knock Knock!
Who's there?
Chester.
Chester who?
Chester minute!

Knock Knock!
Who's there?
Adrian.
Adrian who?
Adrian my hair because it's wet!

Knock Knock!
Who's there?
Aldous.
Aldous who?
Aldous who want to leave the room, put your hand up!

Knock Knock!
Who's there?
Diana.
Diana who?
Diana-mals are restless, let them out of the cage!

Doctor, doctor, I keep thinking I'm in a fast food restaurant. Can you give me anything?

Certainly — eat in or takeaway?

Doctor, doctor, I feel like Tarzan.

Careful — it's a jungle out there.

Why did the king go to the dentist?

To have his teeth crowned.

Doctor, doctor, my kidneys are bad — what should I do?

Take them back to the butcher.

Doctor: Why is your son crying?

Mother: He has four baked beans stuck up his nose.

Doctor: And why is his little sister crying?

Mother: She wants her lunch back.

What kind of bandage do people need after heart surgery?

Ticker tape.

Knock Knock!
Who's there?
Gay.
Gay who?
Gay-topen, that's how the pigs got out!

Knock Knock!
Who's there?
Henrietta.
Henrietta who?
Henrietta hat because he lost a bet!

Knock Knock!
Who's there?
Fiona.
Fiona who?
Fiona of the house, I've come for rent!

Knock Knock!
Who's there?
Bella.
Bella who?
Bella bottom trousers!

396

Knock Knock!
Who's there?
Joe Nameth.
Joe Nameth who?
Joe Nameth not on the door, that's why I knocked!

Knock Knock!
Who's there?
Ivor.
Ivor who?
Ivor fortune!

Knock Knock!
Who's there?
Fiona.
Fiona who?
Fiona had something better to do, I wouldn't be hanging around here!

Knock Knock!
Who's there?
Sigrid.
Sigrid who?
Sigrid service – open up!

How can you tell if you are looking at a police glow-worm?

It has a blue light!

Why are glow-worms good to carry in your bag?

They can lighten your load!

What do you get if you cross a glow-worm with a python?

A fifteen foot strip light that can strangle you to death!

When should you stop for a glow-worm?

When he has a red light!

What is the maggot army called?

The apple corps!

What is a polar bear's favourite band?

Coldplay.

What happened to the glow-worm who was squashed?

He was de-lighted!

What reads and lives in an apple?

A bookworm!

Patient: Be honest — how am I?

Dentist: Your teeth are fine but your gums have to come out.

Patient: Why is the doctor walking in a circle?

Nurse: He's doing his rounds.

Doctor, doctor, I've got a sty in my eye.

You'd better get a pig then.

Doctor, doctor, I keep
dreaming that there are
horrible monsters playing
dominoes under my bed.
What should I do?

Hide the dominoes.

Doctor, doctor, I've
got athlete's foot
on my head.

Why do you say that?

My nose keeps running.

Knock Knock!
Who's there?
Rosa.
Rosa who?
Rosa potatoes grow in our garden!

Knock Knock!
Who's there?
Martin.
Martin who?
Martin of beans won't open!

Knock Knock!
Who's there?
Phineas.
Phineas who?
Phineas thing happened to me on the way home!

Knock Knock!
Who's there?
Celeste.
Celeste who?
Celeste time I lend you money!

Knock Knock!
Who's there?
Tamara.
Tamara who?
Tamara the world!

Knock Knock!
Who's there?
Eddie.
Eddie who?
Eddie-body home?

Knock Knock!
Who's there?
Zena.
Zena who?
Zena stealing my things!

Knock Knock!
Who's there?
Buster.
Buster who?
Buster town please!

What do you call an ant who lives with your great uncle?

Your great-ant.

What do you call an ant with frog's legs?

An ant-phibian.

Where are sheep and cattle sold?

At the stock market.

'Doctor, doctor, I feel like an electric eel!'

'That's shocking!'

Why did the jellyfish blush? Because the sea-weed.

How do eels get around the sea?

They go by octobus.

What do you call a lion that's black and blue all over?

Bruce.

Why is the sky so high?

So birds don't bump their heads.

Doctor: Sorry, we left a sponge in you when we operated last week.

Patient: So that's why I've been feeling so thirsty.

Doctor, doctor, I think I'm turning into a mummy.

Better keep wrapped up then.

Doctor, doctor, is the operation expensive?

Yes, I'm afraid it will cost you an arm and a leg.

Patient: Can you give me something for my baldness?

Doctor: How about a few pounds of pig manure?

Patient: Will that cure it?

Doctor: No, but no one will come near enough to you to notice.

Doctor, doctor, the pills you gave me are for cows.

That's right — you said you wanted to be as strong as an ox.

Knock Knock!
Who's there?
Juliet.
Juliet who?
Juliet the same amount but she's OK!

Knock Knock!
Who's there?
Sadie.
Sadie who?
Sadie end of the joke!

Knock Knock!
Who's there?
Euripedes.
Euripedes who?
Euripedes trousers and you'll pay for a new pair!

Knock Knock!
Who's there?
Robin.
Robin who?
Robin the larder is wrong!

Knock Knock!
Who's there?
Shelly.
Shelly who?
**Shelly con carne –
Mexican food!**

Knock Knock!
Who's there?
Cyril.
Cyril who!
**Cyril pleasure to
meet you again!**

Knock Knock!
Who's there?
Morris.
Morris who?
**Morris in the pot,
help yourself!**

Knock Knock!
Who's there?
John.
John who?
**John me for a cup
of tea!**

Knock Knock!
Who's there?
Toothy.
Toothy who?
Toothy is the day before Wednesday!

Knock Knock!
Who's there?
Drucilla.
Drucilla who?
Drucilla kid you! You might have got hurt!

Knock Knock!
Who's there?
Urlah.
Uriah who?
Keep Uriah on the ball!

Knock Knock!
Who's there?
Athol.
Athol who?
Athol'd my bike so now I have to walk everywhere!

Knock Knock!
Who's there?
Beth.
Beth who?
Beth wishes!

Knock Knock!
Who's there?
Ann.
Ann who?
Ann-onymous!

Knock Knock!
Who's there?
Chad.
Chad who?
Chad to make your acquaintance!

Knock Knock!
Who's there?
Esme.
Esme who?
Esme petticoat hanging out the back?

Doctor, doctor, I don't like all these flies buzzing around my head.

Well, point out the ones you do like and I'll swat the rest.

Doctor, doctor, how can I lose 10 kilos?

Try putting that suitcase down!

Doctor, doctor, call me an ambulance!

You're an ambulance.

Doctor, doctor, my wife thinks she's a motorbike.

Give her these pills and she'll be cured.

But how will I get home?

Doctor, doctor, my little boy keeps biting his nails.

Don't worry, it's quite common.

What, with six-inch rusty ones?

Doctor, doctor, I think I'm a DVD.

I thought I'd seen you before.

Knock Knock!
Who's there?
Noah.
Noah who?
Noah a good place to find more jokes?

Knock Knock!
Who's there?
Stefan.
Stefan who?
Stefan nonsense!

Knock Knock!
Who's there?
Della.
Della who?
Della-katessen!

Knock Knock!
Who's there?
Belinda.
Belinda who?
Belinda church steeple!

Knock Knock!
Who's there?
Evadne.
Evadne who?
**Evadne new
teeth through?**

Knock Knock!
Who's there?
Dick.
Dick who?
**Dick potatoes out
of the ground!**

Knock Knock!
Who's there?
Bill.
Bill who?
Bill-tup area!

Knock Knock!
Who's there?
Miss.
Miss who?
**Miss L. Toe is nice
at Christmas!**

Knock Knock!
Who's there?
Census.
Census who?
Census Saturday we don't have to go to school!

Knock Knock!
Who's there?
Grammar.
Grammar who?
Grammar is my favourite relative!

Knock Knock!
Who's there?
Disaster.
Disaster who?
Disaster be my lucky day!

Knock Knock!
Who's there?
Nettie.
Nettie who?
Nettie as a fruitcake!

Knock Knock!
Who's there?
Sal.
Sal who?
**Sal-ong way
to Tipperary!**

Knock Knock!
Who's there?
Zone.
Zone who?
**Zone shado
scares him!**

Knock Knock!
Who's there?
Miniature.
Miniature who?
**Miniature open
your mouth you
put your foot in it!**

Knock Knock!
Who's there?
Hannah.
Hannah who?
**Hannah partridge
in a pear tree!**

Doctor, doctor, I'm worried about my breathing.

Don't worry — we'll soon find something to stop it.

Patient: Will the doctor be round soon?

Nurse: No, tall and slim as usual.

Doctor, doctor, I've swallowed a watch.

Take this medicine — it'll help you pass the time.

Doctor, doctor, I get so nervous when I drive that I keep bumping into things.

I'm going to send you on a crash course.

Doctor, doctor, I've got a nasty chill — what should I do?

Avoid draughts for a week.

Can I play ludo instead?

Doctor, doctor, I keep dressing up as a French soldier.

You must have Legionnaire's disease.

Knock Knock!
Who's there?
Anna.
Anna who?
Anna-nother thing, how long do I have to wait for you to open up!

Knock Knook!
Who's there?
Tillio.
Tillie who?
Tillie comes home, I'll wait here!

Knock Knock!
Who's there?
Weasel.
Weasel who?
Weasel while you work!

Knock Knock!
Who's there?
Amahl.
Amahl who?
Amahl shook up!

Knock Knock!
Who's there?
Ina Clare.
Ina Clare who?
Ina Clare day you can see for miles!

Knock Knock!
Who's there?
Sis.
Sis who?
Sis anyway to treat a friend?!

Knock Knock!
Who's there?
Emmett.
Emmett who?
Emmett the back door, not the front!

Knock Knock!
Who's there?
Sultan.
Sultan who?
Sultan pepper!

Knock Knock!
Who's there?
Virtue.
Virtue who?
Virtue get your beautiful eyes from?

Knock Knock!
Who's there?
Honda.
Honda who?
Honda the tree!

Knock Knock!
Who's there?
Stepfather.
Stepfather who?
One stepfather and I'll be inside!

Knock Knock!
Who's there?
Formosa.
Formosa who?
Formosa the summer I went on holiday!

422

Knock Knock!
Who's there?
Pharaoh.
Pharaoh who?
Pharaoh-nuff!

Knock Knock!
Who's there?
Geordie.
Geordie who?
Geordie-rectly to jail, do not pass go, do not collect £200.

Knock Knock!
Who's there?
Scold.
Scold who?
Scold outside!

Knock Knock!
Who's there?
Izzy.
Izzy who?
Izzy come, Izzy go!

What did the hypochondriac write on his gravestone?

I TOLD YOU I WAS ILL!

Doctor, doctor, I think I've got a split personality.

Sit down, both of you.

Mother: It's time for your medicine.

Son: I'll run the bath.

Mother: Why?

Son: Because it says 'to be taken in water'.

Doctor: I told you that you were overweight for your height.

Patient: No, no, no — I'm just too short for my weight.

Doctor, doctor, I think I'm turning into a woman.

Well, you are sixteen, Julie.

Doctor, doctor, I keep dreaming about next week's lottery.

Hang on, I'll get a pen.

Knock Knock!
Who's there?
Pizza.
Pizza who?
Pizza cake would be great right now!

Knock Knock!
Who's there?
Eamon.
Eamon who?
Eamon my way out. Do you want to come?

Knock Knock!
Who's there?
Cellar.
Cellar who?
Cellar? No I think it can be repaired!

Knock Knock!
Who's there?
Harriet.
Harriet who?
Harriet all my lunch!

Knock Knock!
Who's there?
Lauren.
Lauren who?
Lauren order!

Knock Knock!
Who's there?
Faye.
Faye who?
Faye Kearings!

Knock Knock!
Who's there?
House.
House who?
Hugh's fine thank you!

Knock Knock!
Who's there?
Delores.
Delores who?
Delores on the side of good people!

Knock Knock!
Who's there?
Barry.
Barry who?
Barry the treasure so no one will find it!

Knock Knock!
Who's there?
Odette.
Odette who?
Odette's a bad sign!

Knock Knock!
Who's there?
Yelp.
Yelp who?
Yelp me! My nose is stuck to the window!

Knock Knock!
Who's there?
Artichoke.
Artichoke who?
Artichoke on his food!

Knock Knock!
Who's there?
Punch.
Punch who?
Not me please!

Knock Knock!
Who's there?
Statue.
Slatue who?
Statue? This is me!

Knock Knock!
Who's there?
Stop-watch.
Stop-watch who?
Stop-watch you're doing right now!

Knock Knock!
Who's there?
Jaws.
Jaws who?
Jaws truly!

Doctor: You've got spotted fever.

Patient: Is it serious?

Doctor: Not if it's spotted in time.

Doctor, doctor, I think I'm a piece of soap.

That story won't wash with me.

Doctor, doctor, I think I'm Bambi.

Oh, you poor dear.

Doctor, doctor,

I keep thinking I'm a toad.

Go on, hop it.

Doctor, doctor, I keep thinking I'm an elevator.

How are you feeling?

Oh, up and down.

Doctor, doctor, I think I need glasses.

Read out these letters please?

Why?

My secretary is off sick.

Doctor, doctor, I think I'm a circus performer.

Stop clowning about.

Knock Knock!
Who's there?
Roland.
Roland who?
**Roland butter
please!**

Knock Knock!
Who's there?
Gilda.
Gilda who?
**Gilda fly that won't
leave me alone!**

Knock Knock!
Who's there?
Alice.
Alice who?
**Alice forgiven,
come back!**

Knock Knock!
Who's there?
Hope.
Hope who?
**Hopefully that
present is for me!**

432

Knock Knock!
Who's there?
Carman.
Carman who?
Carman get it!

Knock Knock!
Who's there?
Santa.
Santa who?
Santa text reminding you I'd be here!

Knock Knock!
Who's there?
Nora.
Nora who?
Nora bone!

Knock Knock!
Who's there?
Argo.
Argo who?
Argo to the beach on holiday!

What is a polygon?
A dead parrot.

What kind of bird
opens doors?

A key-wi.

What do you
get if you cross an
ant with half a pair
of knickers?

A pant.

What do baby
swans dance to?

Cygnet-ure-tunes.

What do you call an old ant?

An antique.

What is a duck's favourite TV show?

The feather forecast.

Where do birds invest their money?

In the stork-market!

Where do blind sparrows go for treatment?

The Birds Eye counter!

435

Doctor, doctor, my son has a nail-biting problem.

Is it serious?

Well, they're not his nails.

Doctor, doctor, I've got holes all over my body.

I'm not surprised — I'm an acupuncturist.

Doctor, doctor, I think I'm a banana.

Go behind the screen and slip out of your clothes.

Doctor, doctor, my son has got a button stuck up his nose. What should I do?

Tell him to breathe through the four little holes.

Doctor, doctor, I think I'm turning into a cricket bat.

You've left me completely stumped.

What happened when the owl lost his voice?

He didn't give a hoot!

What happens when ducks fly upside down?

They quack up.

What do you get if you cross an elephant with some locusts?

I'm not sure, but if they ever swarm, watch out.

What do you get if you cross a rabbit with an elephant?

Big holes in your garden.

What did the fish
say when it swam
into a wall?

'Dam!'

What do you get
if you cross a
woodpecker with a
carrier pigeon?

A bird who knocks
before delivering
its message.

What is
smaller than an
ant's dinner?

An ant's mouth.

Why did the elephant
put his trunk across
the path?

To trip up the ants.

Knock Knock!
Who's there?
Zeke.
Zeke who?
Zeke and ye
shall find!

Knock Knock!
Who's there?
Guinevere.
Guinevere who?
Guinevere going
to tell me?

Knock Knock!
Who's there?
Don.
Don who?
Don just stand
there, say
something!

Knock Knock!
Who's there?
Sherry.
Sherry who?
Sherry dance?

Knock Knock!
Who's there?
Datsun.
Datsun who?
Datsun really old joke!

Knock Knock!
Who's there?
Bernadette.
Bernadette who?
Bernadette all my dinner again!

Knock Knock!
Who's there?
Egypt.
Egypt who?
Egypt my best china plate!

Knock Knock!
Who's there?
Noah.
Noah who?
Noah yes – which one is it?

Doctor, doctor, I feel like going on a long holiday.

Take these.

What are they?

They're my children.

Doctor, doctor, I keep feeling sick.

How bad is it?

Well, it's not my sick.

Doctor, doctor, I keep thinking I'm a slice of bread.

You must stop loafing around.

Doctor, doctor,
I feel like a pile
of old clothes.

Yes, you are
looking a little worn.

Doctor, doctor, I'm
having trouble sleeping.

Maybe it's your bed.

Oh, I'm all right at night
— it's during the day
that I have problems.

Doctor, doctor, I'm a
blood-sucking monster
and I eat doctors.

Ah, well I'm a dentist.

Knock Knock!
Who's there?
Ella.
Ella who?
Ella mann-tree my dear Watson!

Knock Knock!
Who's there?
Ada.
Ada who?
First Ada Kit!

Knock Knock!
Who's there?
John.
John who?
John me for dinner.

Knock Knock!
Who's there?
Owl.
Owl who?
Owl aboard!

Knock Knock!
Who's there?
Yacht.
Yacht who?
Yacht's up Doc?

Knock Knock!
Who's there?
Hal.
Hal who?
Hallo to you too!

Knock Knock!
Who's there?
Tucson.
Tucson who?
Tucson and two daughters are enough kids!

Knock Knock!
Who's there?
Pizza.
Pizza who?
Pizza pie please!

Knock Knock!
Who's there?
Stu.
Stu who?
Stu late to ask questions!

Knock Knock!
Who's there?
Mummy.
Mummy who?
Mummeasles are better so can I come in?

Knock Knock!
Who's there?
Louisana.
Louisana who?
Louisana boyfriend broke up!

Knock Knock!
Who's there?
Socket.
Socket who?
Socket to me!

Knock Knock!
Who's there?
Ooze.
Ooze who?
**Ooze been sleeping
in my bed?**

Knock Knock!
Who's there?
Sophie.
Sophie who?
**Sophie come to the
end of the lesson!**

Knock Knock!
Who's there?
Lilac.
Lilac who?
**Lilac that
and you're
in trouble!**

Knock Knock!
Who's there?
Atlas.
Atlas who?
**Atlas we can
talk properly!**

Doctor, doctor, I keep thinking I'm Napoleon.

How long have you felt like this?

Ever since Waterloo.

Doctor, doctor, my ears keep ringing.

I suggest you change your number.

Doctor, doctor, I think I'm turning into a sweater.

Well, pull over and let's have a look at you.

Doctor, doctor, my wife thinks she is a duck.

Can you bring her in?

No — she's already flown south for the winter.

Doctor, doctor, I think I've been bitten by a vampire.

Drink this glass of water.

Will that make me better?

No, but I'll be able to see if your neck leaks.

Doctor, doctor, I think I've died and become a ghost.

Is there anybody there?

What do you call a pig in a striped shirt and a mask?

A piggy bank robber.

What do you call a musical ladybird?

A hum bug.

What do you get if you cross an octopus with a skunk?

An octopong.

How do you start a jellyfish race?

Get set!

What goes straight up in the air and wobbles?

A jellyfishcopter!

What happened to the dog that fell into a lens-grinding machine?

He made a spectacle of himself.

What happened when the shaggy dog swallowed a teaspoon?

He wasn't able to stir.

What has 2,000 eyes and 4,000 feet?

A thousand dogs.

Knock Knock!
Who's there?
Dennis.
Dennis who?
**Dennis say
I need a filling!**

Knock Knock!
Who's there?
Alaska.
Alaska who?
Alaska my mummy!

Knock Knock!
Who's there?
Moppet.
Moppet who?
**Moppet up before
it gets sticky!**

452

Knock Knock!
Who's there?
Wotsit.
Wotsit who?
Wotsit matter to you?

Knock Knock!
Who's there?
Costa.
Costa who?
Costa lot!

Knock Knock!
Who's there?
Halibut.
Halibut who?
Halibut letting me in on the secret?

Doctor, doctor, I've got carrots growing out of my ears.

How did that happen?

I don't know — I planted potatoes.

Doctor, doctor, I think I'm suffering from déjà vu!

'Didn't I see you yesterday?'

Doctor, doctor, I swallowed a light bulb.

Don't worry, there's a light at the end of the tunnel.

Doctor, doctor,
my brother thinks he's a
piece of chewing gum.

Send him in to see me.

I can't — he's stuck
under a desk.

Doctor, doctor, I've
turned into an ugly
duckling.

I'm not some quack
you know.

Doctor, doctor, I
think I'm a robot.

You must have a
screw loose.

Knock Knock!
Who's there?
Jade.
Jade who?
Jade a whole cake today!

Knock Knock!
Who's there?
Ivan.
Ivan who?
Ivan no idea!

Knock Knock!
Who's there?
Paul Lee.
Paul Lee who?
**Feeling Paul-lee so
I stayed in bed!**

Knock Knock!
Who's there?
Water-skier.
Water-skier who?
Water-skier Dof?
It won't hurt you!

Knock Knock!
Who's there?
Athene.
Athene who?
Athene you about,
haven't I?

Knock Knock!
Who's there?
Dwayne.
Dwayne who?
Dwayne in Spain
falls mainly on
the plain!

Knock Knock!
Who's there?
Victor.
Victor who?
Victor his trousers getting here!

Knock Knock!
Who's there?
Noise.
Noise who?
Noise to see you!

Knock Knock!
Who's there?
Senior.
Senior who?
Senior mother out and let me in!

Knock Knock!
Who's there?
Vanessa.
Vanessa who?
Vanessa you going to grow up?

Knock Knock!
Who's there?
Enid.
Enid who?
Enid some food!

Doctor, doctor, I've lost my memory.

Well, just pay me the £10,000 you owe me and I'll see what I can do.

Doctor, doctor, I've got flowers growing between my toes.

Don't worry — they're just cornflowers.

Doctor, doctor, I've gone blind. What can I do?

Put your crash helmet on the right way round.

Doctor, doctor, I keep getting dizzy spells.

When do they start?

Each time I step off the roundabout.

Doctor, doctor, I can't stop sneezing. What can you give me?

A tissue?

Oh no, it's happening to you as well.

Doctor, doctor, I've only got one tooth left — what should I do?

You'll just have to grin and bear it.

Knock Knock!
Who's there?
Worzel.
Worzel who?
It's upstairs on the left!

Knock Knock!
Who's there?
Marcella.
Marcella who?
Marcella's full of wator!

Knock Knock!
Who's there?
Juanita.
Juanita who?
Juanita 'nother hot dog!

Knock Knock!
Who's there?
Harvey.
Harvey who?
Harvey gonna play this game forever?

Knock Knock!
Who's there?
Kansas.
Kansas who?
Kansas the best way to buy tuna!

Knock Knock!
Who's there?
Fajita.
Fajita who?
Fajita another thing I'm going to be sick!

Knock Knock!
Who's there?
Obi Wan.
Obi Wan who?
**Obi Wan of the good
guys, let me in!**

Knock Knock!
Who's there?
Dad.
Dad who?
**Dad fuel to
the fire!**

Knock Knock!
Who's there?
Paine.
Paine who?
Paine in the neck!

Knock Knock!
Who's there?
Kenneth.
Kenneth who?
**Kenneth little kids
play with you?**

Knock Knock!
Who's there?
Havanna.
Havanna who?
**Havanna wonderful time –
wish you were here!**

Knock Knock!
Who's there?
Organ.
Organ who?
**Organise a party,
it's my birthday!**

Doctor, doctor, my corn's hurting a lot.

Here, put this ointment on it.

What? All over the field.

Doctor, doctor, I think I'm about to lay an egg.

Don't count your chickens before they hatch.

Doctor, doctor, I think I'm turning into a shark.

Don't worry — there's no fin to worry about.

Doctor, doctor, my boyfriend's hand isn't connected to his shoulder. What should I do?

Give him the elbow.

Doctor, doctor, do I need to have a transplant?

I think we should have a heart-to-heart.

Doctor, doctor, My sister thinks she's a seabird.

She'll just have to wait her tern.

Knock Knock!
Who's there?
Dancer.
Dancer who?
Dancer is simple, it's me!

Knock Knock!
Who's there?
Pam.
Pam who?
Pam-per yourself!

Knock Knock!
Who's there?
Fanta.
Fanta who?
Fanta Claus!

Knock Knock!
Who's there?
Ohio.
Ohio who?
Ohio Silver!

Knock Knock!
Who's there?
Dawn.
Dawn who?
**Dawn leave me
out here in
the cold!**

Knock Knock!
Who's there?
Felipe.
Felipe who?
**Felipe bath,
I need a wash!**

Knock Knock!
Who's there?
Doug.
Doug who?
Doug good deeds and you'll go to heaven!

Knock Knock!
Who's there?
Handel.
Handel who?
Handel with care!

Knock Knock!
Who's there?
Lock.
Lock who?
Lock who it is – after all this time!

470

Knock Knock!
Who's there?
Plane.
Plane who?
Plane innocent won't save you!

Knock Knock!
Who's there?
Orest.
Orest who?
Orest that man!

Knock Knock!
Who's there?
Red.
Red who?
Reddy, aim, fire!

Doctor, doctor, I'm turning
into a chameleon.

I think you're just a
little off-colour.

Doctor, doctor,
my face is white
and my nose is
bright red. What
should I do?

Quit clowning
around.

Doctor, doctor, I'm
turning into a bird.

Well, knock me
down with a feather.

Doctor, doctor, I think I'm turning into an ostrich.

I think you need to take your head out of the sand.

Doctor, doctor, I think I'm a hungry puppy.

You're pulling my leg.

Patient: Will you treat me?

Doctor: No, you'll have to pay like everyone else.

Knock Knock!
Who's there?
Crush.
Crush who?
Crush on you!

Knock Knock!
Who's there?
Kitten.
Kitten who?
Kitten the park hit me with a ball!

Knock Knock!
Who's there?
Handsome.
Handsome who?
Handsome sweets through the door!

Which animals are the snootiest?

The ones that live in trees – they look down on all the other creatures.

What do you get if you cross a blind lion with a spiked shoe?

A very cross blind lion.

What did one flea say to the other after a night out?

'Shall we walk home or take a dog?'

Which elephants have the shortest legs?

The smallest ones!

What is a flea's favourite book?

The Itch-hiker's Guide to the Galaxy!

Why did the stupid boy wear a polo neck sweater?

To hide his flea collar!

What is a bear's favourite drink?

Coca-Koala!

What is the difference between a dead bee and a sick gorilla?

One is a hairy beast and the other's a bee deceased.

476

How do you make an elephant laugh?

Tickle its ivories.

How do you hire a teddy bear?

Put him on stilts.

Why was the little bear so spoiled?

Because its mother panda'd to its every whim.

What should you call a bald teddy?

Fred bear.

Dentist: I told you not to swallow.

Patient: Why?

Dentist: That was my last pair of pliers.

What is a medicine dropper?

A doctor with greasy fingers.

Doctor: Your cough sounds much better.

Patient: It should be — I practised all night.

Doctor: Have you ever had an accident?

Farmer: No — never.

Doctor: What about when the bull tossed you over the fence?

Farmer: Ah, the bull did it on purpose.

Doctor, doctor, I get the feeling that nobody cares what I say.

So what?

What fish gets up the river at 100 mph?

A motor pike.

What is black and white and red all over?

A dalmatian with a bad sunburn.

What is taller when it sits down than when it stands up?

A dog.

What is a dog's favourite tree?

The dogwood.